Birds of the Highveld
Peter Ginn

Longman

Longman Zimbabwe (Pvt) Ltd
Tourle Road, Ardbennie, Harare

*Associated companies, branches and
representatives throughout the world*

© P. Ginn and SCNVYO 1972

First published 1972
Fifth impression 1987

ISBN 0 582 60890 2

Printed in Zimbabwe by Mardon Printers (Pvt Limited, Harare

Contents

Introduction

A book of this size is necessarily limited as to the number of species which can be described. This poses all sorts of problems and it is obviously quite impossible to please everybody. In fact it is extremely difficult to please most people most of the time. In drawing up a list from which the final selection was made I have received considerable assistance from a number of ornithologists in Zimbabwe, but the final selection is mine. In making the final choice I have tended towards selecting birds which are commonly found on the plateau, hence the name *Birds of the Highveld*. I hope that a companion volume in which the emphasis will be on the lowveld birds will be produced later.

This book is mainly for the beginner who wishes to watch birds in the field. In this field book I have tried as far as possible to emphasise the field characters of each bird. This immediately raises the problem of what are the field characters of birds. A field character is any feature of the bird which can be observed in the field and must therefore include things such as the habitat, the size and shape of the bird, the colours, and so on. Far too often emphasis is placed on the colours of the various parts of the bird, but when in the field the expert very often makes more use of the shape of the various parts of the bird and its habits rather than the colours.

The basic field character is the habitat. Every species has certain limitations placed on it by the food which it eats and this in turn means that the habitat is usually of great importance. Some species do occur in a wide variety of habitats, but most species are usually limited to one or two habitats although they may occur in others. The occurrence of species outside their normal habitats will obviously occur because birds are highly mobile. Where they occur in unusual circumstances, however, they are merely vagrant and one would not normally expect to find them there.

The book is therefore divided into a series of different habitats and birds are described under the habitat in which they are most likely to be seen by the beginner. The urban and rural garden environments are also described as separate habitats although in many ways they bear ornithological relationships to the surrounding countryside. Many species have adapted more or less to man's artificial environment and as the majority of people who read this book probably live within the urban environment emphasis is placed on this to a certain extent. The House Sparrow has adapted so well that it is only found in association with man's buildings. The swallows on the other hand have taken advantage of the extra nest sites provided by buildings, culverts and bridges to extend their range and quite possibly have increased in numbers. Some species, however, are seldom if ever found within these habitats and one would have to go into the field to observe them. It is noteworthy that, if they are not molested, most species found in association with man tend to become tamer than they are in the wild—the Kurrichane Thrush is an excellent example of this. Where man is prepared to go to the trouble of feeding and supplying drinking water for them, the birds in his garden can become extremely tame. It should be remembered that with the exception of the House Sparrow, which is an introduced species, the birds which are found in towns do occur naturally in certain habitats and these are described under each species.

While the habitat can be considered to be basic to the bird identification, and is thus chosen as the basis for the subdivision of this book, many other characters must also be used and these are briefly summarised in the next chapter.

The birds selected are not necessarily the most common in any particular area, but they are ones which I believe a beginner is likely to find when out looking for birds. I have been forced to omit a number of species which I should have liked to include, but these will be given in the next volume. This is a field book and therefore I have concentrated on field characters as far as possible, and in some cases the choice of a particular species or the omission of another species has been determined by the problems of field identification.

If you wish to obtain more detail about a particular species, I would refer you to Robert's *Birds of South Africa*, revised by McLachlan and Liversidge or to the *African Handbook of Birds*,

Birds of the Southern Third of Africa, by Mackworth-Praed and Grant. Both these books deal with the species occurring in southern Africa in a systematic way and should be available at your nearest library.

Scientific names follow Clancy's *A Catalogue of Birds of the South African Sub-region*, Durban Museum Novitates, 1965-66.

Acknowledgements

I should like to thank the following for help and encouragement in preparing this book:

Mr E. Arnott	Mr C. Laubscher
Mrs S. Arnott	Mr E. Lyons
Mr R. Borrett	Mr G. McIlleron
Mr R. Boulton	Mr W. T. Miller
Mr R. Brooke	Mr W. Nichol
Mr K. Cackett	Mr A. Niven
Mr R. Cook	Mr P. Steyn
Mr A. Kemp	Mr C. Vernon
Mrs M. Kemp	Miss J. Webber

Identification

Looking for birds in Zimbabwe is something which can pose few problems for anybody as we have an abundance of birds available on our very doorsteps. Even in the urban environment there are birds although, where there are no gardens, the variety may be somewhat limited. The problem for the beginner is to learn to identify the birds around him and there is no easy way in which he can do this. It is essential that the beginner look at the birds within each habitat or environment and try to learn something about them and something about their habits.

The identification of birds is carried out through a combination of different factors and the criteria used as the basis of identification will vary according to whether you are studying the bird in the field or in the hand. This book is designed for those people who like to look at their birds in the field in the natural state, although I feel that a beginner can learn a great deal by looking at mounted specimens in a museum or by looking at wild birds which have been tamed and are kept in an aviary. The field characters of birds vary not only from species to species but also from family to family. This means that the beginner must attempt to note down all the characters of the bird in some sort of logical sequence in order that he might be able to identify the bird from a book. You can learn a great deal from an expert when in the field, but you should never merely accept his identification. When a bird is identified you should ask the expert to explain why he identified the bird the way he did. If he can give you three good reasons for his identification then you will learn how to identify this species yourself when you see it at a later date. It is advisable to make a note of these field characters at the time as you will find that it is often impossible to recall them later.

When you begin to identify birds you should do so with the idea in mind that you must first identify the family to which the bird belongs. If you know that the bird you are watching is a dove for instance, you immediately limit your choice to some nine species in Zimbabwe, out of a total of some 600-plus species. Having decided to which family the bird belongs you are then set to identify the species. Further subdivision may take place according to the habitat in which you have observed the bird and this might bring you down to some three or four species and thus make the final identification relatively simple. Unfortunately it is impossible to reach this level in a short time because even the identification of families poses certain problems for the beginner. If you approach the problem systematically, however, you will find that you learn to identify very quickly all the more common families with which you come into contact.

You will find that in most cases the expert is able to identify the family to which a bird belongs even if he can see only a silhouette. In fact, I think that many of our birds can be identified to species level without using any colours at all. Unfortunately the tendency for the beginner, or in fact for most people looking for birds, is to look at the colours instead of looking at other characters which are often of much greater importance. In identifying birds use must be made of a large number of different characteristics of which colour is only one. Thus you should look at the general shape and form of the bird, the shape of the bill, the way it moves, the way it feeds and also the habitat or environment in which it is found. Somebody who has spent some time watching birds soon learns to assess all of these characters simultaneously and therefore comes up with an answer as to the species involved. This is achieved only through experience in the field where the birds may be watched as they feed and so on. When you get home, there is something extremely satisfying in tracking down the identity of a bird seen in the field using notes made at the time of observation. I would stress that the making of mental notes is on the whole unreliable and, if you must make a note, make it in a notebook.

The description of a bird seen in the field could well be made under a series of headings as follows:

1 *A brief description of the habitat.* You do not need to describe the plant species in detail, merely note such features as woodland, water, and so on.

2 *Size and shape of bird.* The selection of a number of well known species is recommended.

In Zimbabwe the following would be a possible selection:

a) Small: House Sparrow or Yellow-eyed Canary.

b) Medium: Laughing Dove or Fork-tailed Drongo.

c) Large: Pied Crow or Crowned Guineafowl.

The bird being studied can then be related to these species, for example: larger than a sparrow but smaller than a dove. The average length of all species described is given below the photographs so that relative size may be determined. The shape may be described as long and thin, short and fat, and so on.

3 *Detailed description of various parts of the bird.* I am inclined to start at the beak and work down through the bird's head, neck, body to the tail, and finally to the legs. This is purely a personal preference, however, and you can tackle this any way you prefer. I think the most important thing is to be systematic about it; thus you should describe the birds in the same way each time.

4 *The colours of the various parts of the bird.* Here it is important to note that one should try to describe the head and neck, and the wings and the tail, in more detail than the rest of the bird, as these are the parts that most often help one in the identification of a particular species. Do not try to use fancy colours unless you are an artist as this merely leads to confusion. The use of basic colours with a few other common colours thrown in should be perfectly adequate.

5 *Attitude.* This is the way the bird sits or stands. You should note whether the bird stands erect or crouches, whether it is sitting on the ground or whether it is in a tree. Does it hang from the tree like a woodpecker? Does it sit across the branch as in most of the perching birds or passerines, or does it sit along the branch as do some nightjars?

6 *Movement.* If the bird moves, does it fly in a direct line from one point to the next? Does it have a rapid or slow wing beat? If the bird is moving on the ground, does it hop or does it walk? If it walks, does it do so with a jerky motion or does it stride along evenly?

7 *Habits.* Things such as the way a bird feeds and, if you can see what it is eating, on what it is feeding can be of very great importance in identifying a particular bird. Any other things that it does should be noted. If you are lucky you may see the

courtship of the bird and this again may help in the identification of the species, although the courtship has not been fully described for many of our birds. As far as possible the 'typical' behaviour is described. However, birds, like all living creatures can do unusual things at times. It is these which add spice to bird watching. They should be recorded at the time of observation and published later if possible.

8 *Voice*. If the bird calls or sings, try to make a note of the call. This is one of the most difficult aspects of bird identification because I find that each person has his own interpretation for a particular bird's call. In many ways it is better to work in reverse, that is, to buy records of bird calls and learn the calls of a particular species. Today there are a number of records of bird calls available in southern Africa and most of these are excellent. In buying records, however, one should look at them to see which species are recorded as some have rather few of the Rhodesian species on them. I find that most people tend to neglect bird calls and yet it is one of the most important aspects of bird identification. Apart from anything else, if you know your bird calls you can move into a new area and fairly quickly assess which species are present. In forests this becomes even more important as many of the species are extremely difficult to see, but give themselves away by their calls. In the case of the cisticolas the identification of species in the field is dependent to a large extent on their calls and the habitat in which they occur.

If you make notes when you see a bird, perhaps following the outline above, then you will be well on your way to identifying the bird by yourself. Even if you cannot identify the bird by yourself, you should be able to identify it with the help of someone who knows something about birds. I would stress however that you must make systematic notes if you hope to have somebody else to identify the bird for you. There is little point in asking an expert to identify a little brown bird which was about the size of your fist, if that is all you can tell him about it.

You can have a lot of fun watching birds at their nests, especially while they have chicks and the adults are coming and going regularly. If you do your bird watching in this way, please remember that the birds are very prone to predation at this stage, so the nest and nest sites should be disturbed as little as possible. If you must move some branches so that you can see the nest, tie them back with a piece of string while you are watching and then release them to hide the nest when you go. You should also bear in mind that the birds are living animals and therefore you should make as much effort as possible not to disturb them if you can help it. If you wish to see what is inside a nest use a mirror stuck on the end of a pole. A mirror on a three metre pole allows you to examine cup shaped nests up to a height of about five metres without having to climb the tree. Woodpeckers' nests may be examined by using a bulb soldered to a piece of flex which is then connected to a battery. The light is pushed down the hole and the contents examined with a mirror.

Watching birds at their nests poses the problem of finding nests in the first place. I have found that beginners are inclined to examine each bush and tree in the hope of finding a nest, but this method is extremely wasteful of both time and energy. Nests are most easily found by watching birds, particularly if the birds are carrying food or nesting material. If you can observe a bird unobtrusively you will eventually see it go to its nest. You should station yourself in such a position that you can watch the general area in which you last saw the bird. Each time you observe it you can move a bit further until the nest is discovered. Obviously this method requires a certain amount of patience, but the rewards are well worth the effort.

When birds are disturbed and they leave the nest, they tend to act in certain ways. If they can they try to sneak away from the nest without being seen, so when moving through the bush keep an eye open for birds which are slipping quietly away. Birds which have been brooding for some time become rather stiff and so if disturbed will often stretch themselves thoroughly when they alight on a branch at some distance from the nest. Finally, many birds become quite agitated when you approach the nest and so give you a good idea of where it is. Unfortunately, even if you know there is a nest in an area you will not necessarily be able to find it. Only experience will tell you what the nest of the species under observation should look like and the situation preferred by this species.

Having discovered a nest, it is vital that while you are watching the birds you disturb them as little as possible. Do not sit near the nest and expect the birds to act in a normal way. If you want to be close to the nest it is essential that you erect a hide in which you can sit concealed. A simple hide may be constructed by placing four rake handles vertically in the ground and putting a nail with the head removed in the top of each. Four broom handles are then drilled so that they can be placed horizontally on top of the rake handles to make a frame. The frame is then covered with canvas or sacking with a hole in the front through which you can observe the bird. This hole should be covered with mosquito netting so that the bird will not see you inside the hide. It is important that the top, back, and sides of the hide be thick enough to stop light from throwing your shadow onto the front of the hide. Nothing frightens a bird more quickly than to see your shadow moving across the front of the hide. If possible have someone accompany you to the hide and walk away when you are safely inside. This will ensure that the bird is less worried by your presence and will return much more quickly to the nest.

If you do not wish to use a hide, seat yourself some distance from the nest and watch from there with a pair of binoculars. In most cases you will need to sit fairly still, or at least in such a position that the bird does not notice you, if you wish the bird to behave normally. If possible make notes of what you see, because you may be the first to observe a particular facet of bird behaviour.

It is obviously possible with experience to identify nests without seeing the bird as each family and, in many cases, each species have distinctive nests. It is, however, essential that confirmation of identification be obtained by observing the bird at the nest because it is not uncommon for some birds to use other birds' nests. For example the Barn Owl often usurps the Hamerkop's nest and a Turtle Dove has been known to lay in a thrush's nest.

Urban environment

The urban environment varies from the areas of tall office blocks with little or no vegetation which are inhabited mainly by birds such as the House Sparrows and Rock Pigeons, through the areas of high-density housing with small gardens to the areas with large gardens which, in fact, in many ways resemble areas of woodland in the field. Contrary to the general impression given by some bird books, the urban environment is an excellent one for birds particularly if gardens are well developed and if people put out food. I think that most people become aware sooner or later that they have birds in their garden, but so often they do not follow this up and learn just what species they have. The birds described in this chapter are ones which could occur in practically any garden within the Zimbabwean towns of the plateau and although they may not be the most common in any particular area they must be considered to be common in many towns. With the exception of the House Sparrow, these birds will also be found in areas where there is no human habitation and in each case the normal environment or habitat for the bird is described.

Bird gardening

Within the urban environment you can attract many more birds to your garden if you spend some time planning your garden. Birds require both shelter and food. Thus in planting the garden you can make provision for certain plants which supply either good cover or food. Generally a garden which has both of these will support a varied bird population. The cover can probably best be supplied by a variety of hedges or shrubs although trees are very important if the size of the garden permits. Do not feel that because your garden is fairly small you cannot attract birds to it, because even the smallest gardens will have birds if there is suitable cover available.

If possible one should leave one corner of the garden to run riot and become heavily overgrown because this supplies an ideal cover for many species of birds. Here again the smaller garden probably cannot accommodate such a corner, but the planting of thick hedges such as Cotoneaster or Bougainvillea will soon make up for any lack of an overgrown corner. Fir trees, which at first glance might appear to be a good source of cover, do not on the whole attract many species of birds and therefore, unless you have a particularly large garden, are probably best omitted. The Banksia Rose which is normally allowed to grow with minimal pruning can form an excellent bird cover and there are many species which seem to like it. One should beware of plants which become too thick, as this will make them unsuitable for most species. The Cypress hedge so favoured by many people in Zimbabwe generally becomes so thick that it merely becomes a haven for Boomslangs and few birds can penetrate it except at the very top. The Jardine's Babbler or Arrow-marked Babbler is perhaps one species which finds a ready nesting site in this type of plant. Apart from the need for protection and cover, these bushes and hedges will supply good nesting sites for many species and therefore are an essential part of the habitats for the birds.

Food should also be catered for when you are planting and therefore if possible plants which supply berries or seeds suitable for the birds should also be planted. Many of the garden plants, for example the Oxford and Cambridge Bush, have berries as well as attractive flowers or foliage. By making use of these you can attract other birds to the garden. The Mulberry tree is probably so well known as to need no mention, but this bush attracts not only the fruit eating birds, but also the insectivorous birds which come to feed on the insects attracted by the fruit. In addition to growing plants which provide food for the birds, one can also feed them. This is dealt with in the section below. Other plants which can be successfully employed for their berries are the Cotoneaster or Hawthorn, the Sunflower and in fact any species of fruit tree will attract birds.

The sunbirds are always attracted to the flowering plants which supply both nectar and also insects which are attracted to the nectar. The sunbirds on the whole prefer the tubular flowers of plants such as the Salvia and Golden Shower, yet they spend a great deal of time probing flowers such as the Hibiscus and Strelitzia. These plants, in addition to being good for attracting the birds, are also extremely attractive and are an asset in any garden.

Bird tables and feeding

If you are prepared to supply food throughout the year you will find that this will bring more birds into your garden and if you supply a variety of food this should also help to bring a variety of birds. I would stress, however, that it is better not to feed at all than to feed erratically. If you once start feeding it is essential that you feed regularly every day because, with the extra food available, the bird population will increase. The birds will welcome any scraps from your table and they are very fond of things like bread in addition to the grains that they are normally fed. The purchase of bird seed enables one to feed the graminivorous birds, but you should also cater for the other birds if possible. Fruit is obviously a great attraction to birds such as the bulbuls and mousebirds. One can feed mealie meal and a variety of birds will in fact eat this particularly if it is put in a bowl with some milk. The barbets and hornbills will eat this throughout the year and I have noticed that many birds such as bulbuls and even the white-eyes will eat the mealie meal during the winter. Broken-up brown bread will attract the weaver birds and bulbuls to a certain extent while dripping is much favoured by robins. Bread if dry should be soaked in milk or water.

It is essential that in any feeding scheme water be provided for the birds both for drinking and bathing purposes. In constructing a bird bath you should make it in such a way that the bath slopes gently from one end down to a deep end which should be some five or six centimetres deep. I have found that if you supply some form of ridge at the deep end birds will generally sit on this to drink and go in from the shallow end when they want to bath. It is essential that the floor of the bird bath be made rough enough so that the birds do not slip when they walk into the water. The sloping bath enables birds to walk in to whatever depth they prefer and thus does not preclude its use by any of the species which are likely to frequent it. Here again, once you have started putting water out it is essential that the water be provided every day. One of the most effective ways of attracting birds is to have water dripping into the bird bath from about fifty centimetres above the water level. Birds do not seem to be able to resist this type of drip.

The construction and maintenance of a bird table and bird bath requires comparatively little work and can be easily co-ordinated into the development of a garden. There are, however, a number of points which should be borne in mind when setting up your bird bath and bird table:

1 Make sure that there is some form of cover nearby to which the birds can fly at the first sign of danger. Ensure that this cover is such that it cannot harbour a cat waiting to pounce on the birds while they are on the bird table or bird bath. Usually a bush or tree near the bird table with the undergrowth kept well clear would be sufficient.

2 When setting up the bird table and bird bath do not put them on the ground. Most birds prefer to be some distance above the ground so as to have a better view or look-out for danger. I have found that a height of between 50 and 150 centimetres is usually acceptable to most species. There are, however, certain species which prefer feeding on the ground and you might therefore throw some seed on the ground below the bird table.

3 The bird table should have some means of draining after rain, unless you are going to build a roof over the bird table to protect the food. Unfortunately the drain hole usually becomes blocked with seed or bits of bread which have expanded after becoming wet. This problem can be overcome by having a piece of gauze under the food area, but this does not make the bird table particularly attractive.

4 Most birds appreciate having some form of perch above the bird table so that they do not need to fly from cover directly onto the bird table. If selected carefully these perches provide ideal perches for bird photography which is easily carried out under these conditions. Finally I would stress that birds will not come to your bird table the first day you put out food so do not be despondent if at first you do not attract many birds. Persevere and in time you will probably find that you have more birds than you can afford to feed. I would suggest that when you reach this stage you put out a certain amount of food regularly at a certain time and then the birds will adapt to this amount of food. The biggest advantage of having a bird table lies in the fact that

the birds become relatively tame and can be easily studied while they are at the table. Therefore, if possible, you should locate the table where you can see it clearly from one of the windows in the house. At first you may find that it is necessary to draw the curtains in the room, but later you will find that the birds become so used to your presence that they will allow you to watch them through the open window.

Descriptions of birds in urban areas

The following descriptions are made to help you identify the birds in your garden and should be used in conjunction with the coloured plates and line drawings. The numbers are those used in Robert's *Birds of South Africa* so that if you wish to obtain more detail on a particular species you can refer to this book as well. No attempt to give a full description of the bird or all its habits is made, but in each case the field characters, i.e. those features which are clearly identifiable in the field and which are an aid to identification, are given.

1 RED-EYED DOVE (R.314)
Plate 11   *STREPTOPELIA SEMITORQUATA*

Field characters: The Red-eyed Dove is the largest of our doves, with the collar on the hind neck. Like all doves it has a rather cylindrical beak which does not appear to taper very much towards the end. The most important field character however is the call which may be rendered as, 'Wuc-wuc- wu-gu-du'. This may also be rendered, 'Coo-coo-cook-KOO-kuk' with the accent on the second last syllable. The bird is much darker than the Cape Turtle Dove and the end of the tail is dark grey rather than white. When alighting the bird gives a rather mewing 'Kree' call. The red eye can be seen if one is close enough to the bird, but on the whole cannot be considered as a good or reliable field character. The large size and generally dark appearance with the paler crown should serve to identify this dove even if it does not call.

Distribution: The Red-eyed Dove occurs over much of Zimbabwe wherever suitable woodland or light forest occurs. It is a bird of the riverine forests and the heavier brachystegia woodland but has adapted itself well to urban conditions and is found in gardens both in the towns and in the country. It will occur in gardens only where there are sufficient trees and it often replaces the Cape Turtle Dove when trees planted in gardens mature. It can become quite common although usually you find that the birds occur in pairs rather than large numbers.

Notes: The Red-eyed Dove comes readily to seed placed on bird tables and may thus be studied quite easily. The nest is the typical dove platform of thin twigs or sticks which is usually placed near the centre of a fairly thick bush or tree. The nest may be fairly low, but is usually between 2,5 and 4 metres above the ground. The eggs are plain white and are somewhat larger than those of the other doves which occur in Zimbabwe. Like the Cape Turtle Dove, the Red-eyed Dove has a soaring display flight in which it rises or towers upwards with clapping wings and then planes downwards with the wings held out rather stiffly. The Red-eyed Dove feeds on both seeds and berries where these are available and it usually needs to drink twice each day.

2 LAUGHING DOVE (R.317)
Plate 27   *STREPTOPELIA SENEGALENSIS*

Field characters: The Laughing Dove is in many ways similar to the Cape Turtle Dove, but it lacks the ring or collar on the back of the neck, and the chest has a rather spotted look and is generally reddish in colour. This can be clearly seen in the photograph on plate 27. The call is a fairly soft, bubbling five syllable one which may be rendered as 'Coo-roo-coo-kuk-coo'.

Distribution: The Laughing Dove occurs over much of Zimbabwe although it does not commonly occur in the areas of better developed brachystegia. It has adapted itself very well to towns and is undoubtedly the most common dove in urban areas. It is seldom seen above about 1 500 to 1 700 metres and is therefore rare in the Eastern Districts.

Notes: This species is readily attracted to bird tables where seed is put out and has therefore become familiar to most people living in the urban areas of Zimbabwe. In these areas it has become domineering and therefore tends to control groups gathered at bird tables. It is certainly not a 'bird of peace' under these circumstances. The nest is rather a flimsy one even by doves' standards. The Laughing Dove will breed throughout the year although most of the breeding takes place in early summer. It lives essentially on seeds which are collected on the ground and therefore it must drink regularly and will be attracted to bird baths.

3 PALM SWIFT (R.387)　　　*CYPSIURUS PARVUS*
Plate 7

Field characters: This small swift is wholly grey in colour. The wings are noticeably long and pointed, and the tail which has long outer feathers is usually carried closed and therefore appears to be very pointed.

Distribution: The Palm Swift is found throughout Zimbabwe, but is generally restricted to areas where palm trees occur.

Notes: The Palm Swift builds its nest in the dead leaves of the palm tree, but in recent years has been recorded as breeding under bridges or in buildings such as the water tower at Lake McIlwaine where the picture shown on plate 7 was taken. These swifts are extremely common and very noticeable along the lines of palm trees in Julius Nyerere Way in Harare. Small groups often occur at isolated palms great distances from the next group. The eggs are glued to the nest with saliva and the chicks grip the nest so tightly that it is extremely difficult to remove them. The adults feed on the wing, chasing insects at high speed.

4 RED-FACED MOUSEBIRD (R.392) *COLIUS INDICUS*
Plate 11

Field characters: The long, thin tail and rapid flight serve to identify this species when it flies overhead. These mousebirds normally occur in small flocks and parties, and the birds within the party keep in touch with a clear melodious whistle 'Pee-wee-wee' or 'Free-wee-wee'. If a good view of the bird is obtained the red face is very obvious as is shown in the photograph on plate 11. Overall, the colouring is a light grey with a paler grey back, and in moving through the bushes the birds creep around somewhat resembling mice with their long, stiff tails.

Distribution: The Red-faced Mousebird may occur anywhere in Zimbabwe, but, apart from Harare, it is not generally very common along the higher parts of the plateau. It seems to favour the drier areas and areas where there are patches of thornveld. It has been attracted to towns by the numerous fruit trees planted in gardens and it may become a pest where deciduous fruits are grown.

Notes: Like all the mousebirds, the Red-faced has a strong bill which is used to tear open fruit in order to get at the pulp and it can cause considerable destruction. When fruit is placed on bird tables, mousebirds often become complete pests as they devour most of the fruit before any of the other birds get a chance to have any. They nest throughout the rains, but most of the nesting is during the early summer. The nest is a rather untidy mass of sticks, many of which are thorny, and the nest is then well lined with fine vegetable down, pieces of wool, or other soft material. The eggs are interesting in that they are usually rather rough and dull but have beautiful russet or red scrolls mainly at the thick end. The Red-faced Mousebird is a fairly strong, fast flier and when disturbed the flock will move off at high speed for some considerable distance before diving into the middle of a bush or tree. Usually these birds make their way to the top of a tree before launching themselves off to fly to the next one.

5 PIED CROW (R.522)   *CORVUS ALBA*

Field characters: The white belly serves to distinguish this crow both in flight and on the ground, and the harsh cries as it flies overhead immediately draw attention to this species. The Pied Crow has become very common in many of the urban centres and frequently can be seen flying over Harare.

Distribution: The Pied Crow may be found over most of Zimbabwe although it seems to be absent in the extreme south and north-west. It is usually associated with human habitation where it has become a first class scavenger. Generally not found in the areas which are forested or very well wooded, the Pied Crow tends to be somewhat localised in its distribution.

Notes: The Pied Crow may occur in pairs or singly, particularly in the breeding season of early summer, or more commonly in small to large flocks. In Harare very large flocks may be noted particularly at favourite roosts. It has adapted very successfully to man's expansion through Africa and may well be extending its own range. The call is a very loud, harsh croak which is uttered both while flying overhead and while sitting on a perch. The nest is a mass of sticks usually placed high up in a tree, this species being one of the few which has found the gum tree a suitable nesting tree. It is parasitised by the Great Spotted Cuckoo which may lay up to thirteen eggs in the crow's nest, but one or two is the normal number. The young cuckoos do not eject the young crows being reared with them.

6 BLACK-EYED BULBUL (R.545)
Plate 29 *PYCNONOTUS BARBATUS*

Field characters: The Black-eyed Bulbul or Toppie has a slight crest of black feathers which contrasts with the rather drab brown of the rest of the bird. The yellow under-tail coverts are very distinctive if seen. The call is a two syllable 'Chit-chit' and may be repeated over and over. It also has a rather longer call which may be rendered 'Come back to Calcutta' and when a number of them get together, or the bird becomes excited, it may chatter very loudly indeed thus drawing attention to itself.

Distribution: The Black-eyed Bulbul is found throughout the Zimbabwean countryside although it is not normally found in forested areas. In the driest parts of Zimbabwe it becomes more local as it seems to be restricted to the areas where water or denser vegetation occur.

Notes: The Toppie will feed on almost any sort of fruit or berries and also eats insects, particularly termites, when available. I feel that the Toppie is one of the 'cleverest' of the Zimbabwean birds and it seems to be able to thrive within the urban environment where most other species are eliminated by cats. Certainly bulbuls which are reared from young chicks make very good pets and show a high degree of 'intelligence'. They are rather noisy birds and are always ready to mob a snake or bird of prey, and in this respect may be considered to be very useful as they draw attention to snakes in the garden. Unfortunately they are also somewhat destructive in fruit orchards where they may consume considerable quantities of soft fruit. The bulbuls nest throughout the year although winter nesting is unusual and the bulk of nesting obviously takes place during the early summer and during the early rains. The nest is usually very cleverly concealed, often in quite low bushes or trees. They are very good at keeping the location of the nest a secret even when feeding chicks. They will come readily to the bird table for fruit and mealie meal and are regular visitors to my bird bath at home.

7 HEUGLIN'S ROBIN (R.580)   *COSSYPHA HEUGLINI*
Plate 13

Field characters: Heuglin's Robin usually draws attention to itself by its beautiful song. It is one of the best songsters in Zimbabwe and may be heard calling from the depths of a thick bush or hedge. The call usually rises to a crescendo which helps to identify it. When seen the white eye stripe is probably the most striking feature, but the orange tail and rump which are clearly visible when the bird flies away are useful aids to identification. Like all robins it often cocks its tail in the air and this action is shown in the photograph on plate 13.

Distribution: It can occur almost anywhere in Zimbabwe except the higher and forested parts of the Eastern Districts where it is replaced by the Cape and Natal Robins. It is a bird of the denser riverine growth but has probably extended its range considerably where gardens offer suitable habitat for it. I have noticed that in certain gardens Heuglin's Robin appears where there is sufficient dense cover for it and soon disappears if this cover is cut back.

Notes: Heuglin's Robin is a rather shy bird which usually makes its presence felt by its song. It will come to feed at the bird table, however, and, like all robins with which I have had experience, it is very fond of dripping. Soon after dawn and after dusk the robins may venture forth from their cover and they may then be seen running around on the ground. The song is most often heard early in the morning or late in the evening but the birds may sing at any time of the day and at any time of the year. The birds usually nest in the summer making a comparatively small cup in a large mass of loose material which makes it difficult to spot in the thick cover.

8 FISCAL SHRIKE (R.707)   *LANIUS COLLARIS*
Plate 13

Field characters: This black and white shrike has a noticeably hooked bill, but in the field probably the most noticeable characteristic is its habit of sitting on a prominent perch from which it pounces on insects on the ground below. When flying from one perch to another it drops down and flies along close to the ground before swooping up onto another perch. The white V on the black back, if visible, helps to identify this species.

Distribution: The Fiscal Shrike is found in park-like country, that is areas with scattered bushes and perhaps trees in grassland. It may occur in light woodland and is often found in gardens particularly where there are large lawns. It occurs over most of Zimbabwe being absent only in the drier areas.

Notes: The Fiscal Shrike is a very bold and aggressive bird and may often be seen chasing other birds in the garden. When doing so it comes down from its perch in a rather planing flight, then chases the smaller birds through the bushes and trees. It will not hesitate to take on large birds of prey if these come anywhere near its nest. It is also attracted to parties of birds mobbing snakes. Unfortunately the Fiscal Shrike tends to chase birds in aviaries or cages and has been known to kill birds in small cages by catching them through the wire. However it does a tremendous amount of good around the garden as it is essentially insectivorous and can help to keep the pests in the garden at a reasonable level. It calls from prominent perches, a rather grating series of warbles and calls usually interspersed with clear whistles many of which are obviously attempts at mimicking other birds and noises heard around the area. The Fiscal Shrike is one of the shrikes which stick insects on thorns forming a sort of larder. The Boubou Shrike is also known to do this. The Fiscal and Boubou Shrikes are mutually exclusive as they have completely different habitat requirements.

9 BOUBOU SHRIKE (R.709) *LANIARIUS FERRUGINEUS*

Field characters: Although superficially similar to the Fiscal Shrike, the Boubou Shrike is a much larger and heavier bird. It has completely different habits as it normally creeps around through the bushes searching for food, not sitting on a prominent perch like the Fiscal Shrike. The white on the wings is not nearly as clearly defined although it does also form a V of sorts on the back. The call is quite distinctive being a two syllable whistle 'Bo-bo'. When calling in duet the first bird whistles 'Bo' and the other answers 'Tsck' whereupon the first bird then calls 'Bo' again. The call often attracts you to the bird as it is not often seen, preferring the thicker cover. Boubou Shrikes do become quite tame in gardens, however.

Distribution: They may occur anywhere in Zimbabwe provided suitable habitat is present. Thus you can say that the distribution is determined by the presence of thick cover, usually along rivers in the natural state, but many gardens with thick hedges and Bougainvillea bushes are ideal for the Boubou Shrike and they have therefore moved into both urban and rural gardens.

Notes: The Boubou Shrike is completely insectivorous and spends a considerable amount of time foraging both within bushes and also on the ground looking for insects. Compared with the nest of the Fiscal Shrike the Boubou Shrike's nest is small and flimsy as can be seen in the illustration on page 21. It is made almost entirely of fine rootlets and twigs, and the eggs can usually be seen from underneath.

10 WHITE-BROWED SPARROW WEAVER (R.780)
PLOCEPASSER MAHALI

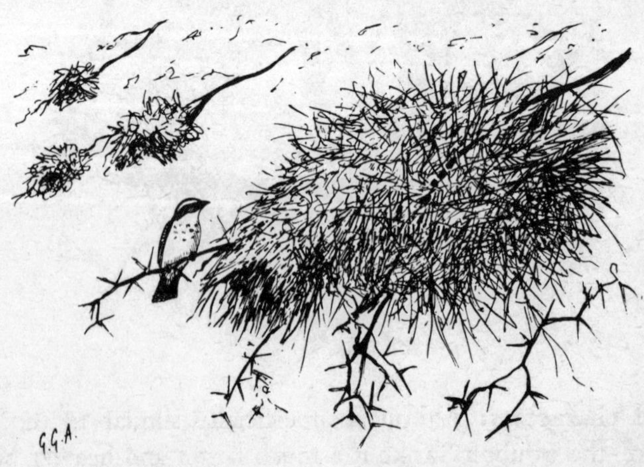

Field characters: I think that without doubt the feature of this species which is most obvious in the field is the nest. The grass nests placed near the outer edge of a thorn bush are very obvious, looking like bunches of grass which have been thrown up into the tree. They are usually on the west side of the tree. The birds go round in small parties which chatter incessantly and thereby draw attention to themselves. They are rather dull being merely white and brown, the white rump and eyebrow being very noticeable in the field when the bird moves around.

Distribution: White-browed Sparrow Weavers are largely associated with the acacia veld and are therefore more typical of the western part of Zimbabwe. They extend eastwards about as far as Chegutu where their nests may be seen along the side of the road. They are common in Bulawayo.

Notes: The nests are very interesting in that they are used throughout the year for roosting and at this stage they have two entrances facing downwards. During the breeding season one entrance is closed thus forming a bowl for the eggs and chicks. The stiff grass stalks from which the nests are made are built in such a way that they stick out at all angles and form the tunnel at the entrance. This would appear to be a deterrent to predation as it makes the nests more difficult to enter. The White-browed Sparrow Weaver spends a lot of time running around on the ground searching for food, but flies into the trees at the first sign of danger. It has become particularly abundant in Bulawayo where the nests may be seen in any areas where acacia is present.

11 HOUSE SPARROW (R.784)   *PASSER DOMESTICUS*
Plate 14

Field characters: The House Sparrow has a distinctive hopping movement on the ground which helps to distinguish it from many similar birds in southern Africa. The male has a black bib which is usually very obvious, but the female lacks this.

Distribution: This bird has spread right across Zimbabwe over the last ten or fifteen years and may now occur in any town and farm throughout the country. It is restricted to settlement and will not be found away from houses and buildings.

Notes: The House Sparrow can become very tame and therefore it is usually well known where it occurs. The birds nest under the eaves of houses or other buildings and come very readily to feed on scraps thrown out from the kitchen or on seed at a bird table. The birds keep in touch with a rather penetrating cheep or whistle and this usually draws attention to them.

12 BRONZE MANNIKIN (R.823)
Plate 1 *SPERMESTES CUCULLATUS*

Field characters: Bronze Mannikins usually go round in small to large flocks and one of the most typical features of this species is the way in which they drop down onto the ground appearing to be falling leaves. Once on the ground they hop around search-ing for seed. If a good view is obtained, the barring on the rump and flanks help in the identification of what is otherwise a rather plain black and white little bird. If the light is right, iridescence is very obvious on the shoulder. The young of this species are plain brown and apart from size do not resemble the adults. When disturbed the whole flock whirrs up into the nearest tree.

Distribution: This species is mainly confined to the eastern half of Zimbabwe although it may occur in the west where suitable habitat is found. They prefer moister open bush and grassland but are attracted to gardens both in urban and rural areas. They do not occur in pure grassland as they like trees for breeding and also as a retreat in case of danger.

Notes: The Bronze Mannikin is readily attracted to bird tables where large numbers may gather to feed on small grain put out. It becomes very tame and allows you to approach quite closely to the bird table while it is feeding. The nest of fine grass stems is a small ball with an entrance to the side facing upwards and is placed near the outside of a tree, usually some height above the ground. In the wild, you usually find Bronze Mannikins sitting on grass stems which they move up feeding on the seeds. The birds will often sit close to one another on a perch, this being particularly noticeable on wires. They appear to cuddle up to one another and there is a continual shuffling and movement within the group as those on the outside try to move in towards the centre. They twitter continuously while doing this.

13 JAMESON'S FIREFINCH (R.835)
Plate 2   *LAGONOSTICTA RHODOPAREIA*

Field characters: Like the Bronze Mannikins, firefinches will often be seen hopping around on the lawn looking for grass seeds. Their red colour, together with the fact that they tend to stay near to cover and in fact prefer to hop around under bushes, serves to distinguish firefinches from mannikins. The white spots are visible only at close range and are not a good field character. Where the Red-billed Firefinch occurs, it is distinguished from Jameson's by its red bill. The Jameson's has a navy blue bill.

Distribution: It occurs throughout Zimbabwe except in the extreme east, where it may be replaced by the Blue-billed Firefinch, and possibly not in the very dry areas of the south-west. It favours thick bush and scrub particularly along rivers but is very partial to gardens both in towns and in the country.

Notes: Jameson's Firefinch will come very readily to a bird table on which small seed such as munga is put out and, like the Bronze Mannikin, becomes very tame in time. Where the Red-billed Firefinch also occurs the two species may join together in the same flock. Where there is thorn scrub Jameson's Firefinch may become very common and in gardens where seed is put out they may also build up into quite large flocks. The nest is a small ball of grass usually placed fairly near the ground in the middle of a bush which has grass growing through it.

14 BLUE WAXBILL (R.839)
Plate 28   *URAEGINTHUS ANGOLENSIS*

Field characters: The powder blue colour and rather longer tail tend to distinguish this small species. The Blue Waxbill in the field appears to be always on the move. It has jerky movements as it hops around from place to place.

Distribution: The Blue Waxbill occurs throughout Zimbabwe apart from the highest parts of the Eastern Districts. It is probably a bird of the thornveld, but has adapted to towns and has therefore become very common in most urban areas in Zimbabwe.

Notes: Once again it is a seed eating bird which comes very readily to the bird table and therefore enables you to study it quite easily. It also needs to drink regularly and makes frequent trips to the bird bath. In the warmer weather it spends a considerable amount of time bathing. The nests are usually very easy to see as the birds seem to make little attempt to conceal them, but very often the nest is placed near that of wasps or hornets and these must serve to protect the nest to a certain extent. The nest itself, like that of the other waxbills, is a ball of grass with the entrance pointing upwards on one side. The Blue Waxbill can become very tame indeed and is often caught by cats.

Rural gardens

Rural gardens are in many ways very similar to those in urban areas but have the great advantage of being in immediate contact with the surrounding countryside. This means that while certain species will normally occur in the rural gardens of which the ones described below are a selection, almost any bird which is found in the surrounding areas can turn up in a rural garden. Once again the rural garden can be developed to attract a greater number of birds, but even without this you will find that because there is normally water available throughout the year, you do find a greater concentration of birds in the garden than in the surrounding areas. I think that probably the water supply is the basic requirement and a bird bath situated in a position where it can be seen from the house can lead to excellent views of the birds of the area.

Rural gardens obviously vary tremendously according to whether the owners are interested in maintaining a garden, but in most cases there will be sufficient thick bush and hedges to attract species like Heuglin's Robin. Where woodlands are available nearby and where there are a reasonable number of trees in the garden you can expect to find species like the Paradise Flycatcher and Black-collared Barbet. The presence of flowers, particularly those with the bell shaped or tubular blooms, will attract the sunbirds. The Scarlet-chested Sunbird in particular has become a very common sight in many rural gardens. One of the most interesting features is that today it often builds its nests on creepers or other plants growing right up against a building. The soft ground under trees in gardens will attract Kurrichane Thrushes and these are often seen scratching around in the fallen leaves. It is interesting that they can become extremely tame in a garden if unmolested, whereas in the wild they tend to be rather wary birds. If you are lucky the Wire-tailed Swallow may nest under the eaves or against the wall of a verandah. I have even seen one building a nest inside a house in the passageway because the front door was nearly always left open during the day.

The notes on bird gardening and the attracting of birds to your garden mentioned in the chapter on urban environment apply equally to the rural garden, and anybody living in the country who is interested in attracting the birds can do so very easily merely by supplying suitable food, water, and cover. I would stress that the presence of food and water by themselves is generally not sufficient to attract birds. The growing of suitable plants to supply cover is at least as important as the other two. Equally the persistent use of pesticides to control insects in the garden is as detrimental to the bird life as it is anywhere else. Birds are in fact extremely efficient insect eaters and you should take care that you do not harm them by the application of pesticides. In fact, by attracting the right sort of bird you can probably have the birds control the insects far more effectively than you can with pesticides. Where pesticides must be used, the types which are not toxic to warm blooded animals should be used if possible.

15 AFRICAN HOOPOE (R.418)   *UPUPA EPOPS*
Plate 5

Field characters: The crest and the long, slightly down-curved bill combined with the black, white, and orange plumage readily distinguish the African Hoopoe. In flight the bird appears to be labouring somewhat and it is not a particularly strong flier, having rather a heavy flapping motion. The female is somewhat duller than the male but otherwise very similar. The call is also a good guide to identification being a rather ventriloquial 'Hoop-hoop' or 'Hoop-hoop-hoop'. During the early part of the breeding season the bird calls continually.

Distribution: The African Hoopoe occurs throughout Zimbabwe wherever open areas are found. It has adapted well to man's gardens finding lawns ideal hunting grounds.

Notes: Although the hoopoe is resident at lower levels, it is present on the higher parts of the plateau only during the summer months. The birds appear during August or September and nesting commences almost immediately. The nest is placed in a hole in the ground or under the eaves of a house. Once the

12   Bronze Mannikin
      4″/100 mm   *Bill Nichol*

19   Bar-throated Apalis
      5″/125 mm   *Peter Ginn*

Plate 1

23   Lesser Double-collared Sunbird ♂
      5″/125 mm   *Bill Nichol*

23   Lesser Double-collared Sunbird ♀
      4½″/112 mm   *Peter Ginn*

13   Jameson's Firefinch ♂
4½″/110 mm   *Peter Ginn*

27   Yellow-eyed Canary
4½″/112 mm   *Peter Ginn*

Plate 2

26   Pin-tailed Whydah ♂ Br
12″/300 mm   *Cyril Laubscher*

26   Pin-tailed Whydah ♀
5″/125 mm   *Peter Ginn*

24 Scarlet-chested Sunbird ♂
6″/150 mm   *Bill Nichol*

24 Scarlet-chested Sunbird ♀
5″/125 mm   *Peter Ginn*

Plate 3

25 Yellow White-eye
4″/100 mm   *Peter Ginn*

28 Streaky-headed Seed-eater
6″/150 mm   *Peter Ginn*

40   Hamerkop   22″/550 mm   *Bill Nichol*

61   Black and Yellow-billed Kites   22″/550 mm   *W. T. Miller*

52   Crowned Cranes   42″/1 050 mm   *Cyril Laubscher*

15   African Hoopoe
11″/275 mm   *Peter Ginn*

Black-collared Barbet
8″/200 mm   *Cyril Laubscher*

Plate 5

18   Kurrichane Thrush
9″/225 mm   *Meg Kemp*

Paradise Flycatcher ♂
9″/225 mm   *Bill Nichol*

36 Moorhen
13"/325 mm   *Bill Nichol*

37 Red-knobbed Coot
17"/425 mm   *Meg Kemp*

Plate 6

38 African Jacana
11"/275 mm   *Bill Nichol*

48 Pied Kingfisher ♂ and ♀
11"/275 mm   *Bill Nichol*

29 Cape Dabchick
6″/150 mm   *Bill Nichol*

55 Yellow-throated Longclaw
8″/200 mm   *Peter Ginn*

Plate 7

49 Malachite Kingfisher
5½″/137 mm   *Bill Nichol*

3 Palm Swift
7″/175 mm   *Bill Nichol*

30 Reed Cormorant
23″/575 mm   *Bill Nichol*

31 Darter
31″/775 mm   *Bill Nichol*

Plate 8

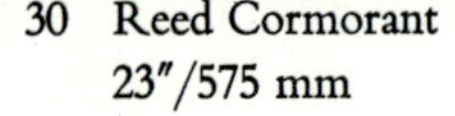

41 Egyptian Goose
28″/700 mm   *Peter Ginn*

33 Knob-billed Duck ♂
31″/775 mm   *Peter Steyn*

chicks have hatched the adults run a shuttle service with grubs and cutworms with which to feed them. While walking around, the hoopoe usually raises and lowers its crest. The male also feeds the female while she is incubating the eggs. As the hoopoes consume vast numbers of grubs they are birds which are to be encouraged in the garden. I suspect that like most insect eating birds they suffer from pesticides used in the garden.

16 BLACK-COLLARED BARBET (R.431)
Plate 5   *LYBIUS TORQUATUS*

Field characters: The red head and face and very large heavy bill distinguish this barbet from most other birds. The call is also very distinctive and as the birds call throughout the year this is usually a useful field character. The call may be rendered as follows: a rather harsh grating warm up followed by a very musical 'Clink-collar, clink-collar, clink-collar', repeated five or six times. The call is a duet between two birds and they usually select a high perch from which to call. The name is derived from the dark black collar surrounding the red head which is clearly shown in the photograph on plate 5.

Distribution: The Black-collared Barbet is found throughout Zimbabwe in suitable woodlands although mopane does not seem to be favoured.

Notes: The Black-collared Barbet is attracted to gardens by the fruit trees, but may also be attracted artificially where these do not occur by the hanging up of suitable nest boxes, preferably old barbets' nests collected in the veld. It will feed on fruit at the bird table but does not seem to be particularly attracted to it. The birds excavate the nest during the non-breeding season and they are extremely destructive in that they continue to enlarge the nest cavity throughout the year which eventually results in the whole branch collapsing. They will excavate the nest in the hardest timber although it must of course be dead. They are parasitised by the Lesser Honeyguide, whose chicks kill the young barbets with the sharp hooks on the tips of the bill. These tips disappear soon after hatching.

17 WIRE-TAILED SWALLOW (R.496)
Plate 30   *HIRUNDO SMITHII*

Field characters: Like all the other hirundines the Wire-tailed Swallow has a blue back and a forked tail. The bird is plain white below with a dusky bar through the vent. The top of the head is red, but this is not always very obvious when the bird is in flight. When seen at close quarters, however, this feature is very clear. It is a comparatively small swallow and in the case of the adults the outer tail feathers are very long and thin as can be seen in the photograph on plate 30.

Distribution: It occurs throughout Zimbabwe, but is common only below 1 300 metres, where it is resident. Above 1 300 metres it is generally rather scarce. The Wire-tailed Swallow is markedly associated with rivers and buildings where there is permanent water.

Notes: The Wire-tailed Swallow builds a half cup shaped nest placed on the wall near the roof of a verandah or under a culvert and is commonly associated with buildings as a result. Many breed throughout the summer, but particularly in early and late summer. Because it is so often associated with farm buildings it is one of the swallows which is most often noticed by people in the country and it becomes extremely tame, coming to the nest even while people are sitting on the verandah. It has therefore become a great favourite with many Zimbabwean farmers.

Swift

Swallow

The diagram shows the differences between swifts and swallows in flight.

18 KURRICHANE THRUSH (R.552)
Plate 5 *TURDUS LIBONYANUS*

Field characters: In the garden the Kurrichane Thrush becomes very tame and may therefore be studied relatively easily. In the wild, however, the Kurrichane Thrush is a wary bird. When seen clearly the orange beak with the streaks down the side of the throat are characteristic and the orange breast and flanks with the grey back are usually seen (see photograph on plate 5). The way it runs at great speed across the ground, stopping suddenly to peck at some insect, is also characteristic.

Distribution: Apart from the forested areas of the Eastern Districts, where it is replaced by the Olive Thrush, the Kurrichane Thrush may be found throughout Zimbabwe wherever suitable woodland occurs. It is a woodland species which is thus restricted to riparian growth in the drier areas, but is widespread elsewhere. It is attracted to gardens probably because of the soft dug-over flower beds where it finds plenty of insects.

Notes: The Kurrichane Thrush is essentially insectivorous, but in Zimbabwe at least it is extremely fond of mulberries when these are available. During the mulberry season it eats a lot of the fruit which has dropped off the trees and is lying on the ground. The Kurrichane Thrush probably also collects insects attracted to this fruit, but the droppings bear evidence to the amount of fruit eaten. The nest is usually put in the fork of a tree and is a large mass of twigs, mud, and so on, camouflaged to a greater or lesser extent with dry materials. On the ground the bird runs with the head held rather low and the tail up and then stops suddenly, lifting the head to look around for danger. When feeding, the bird flicks leaves and other debris aside with rapid sideways movements of the bill. It then peers at the ground before pecking or flicking again.

19 BAR-THROATED APALIS (R.622)
Plate 1 *APALIS THORACICA*

Field characters: The Bar-throated Apalis usually draws attention to itself by its loud calls which, although slightly variable, have the essential 'Chip-chip-chip' call interspersed with the other notes. The bird itself has a rather greenish grey back, and a white throat and belly except for the black collar from which it derives its name. This is clearly seen in the photograph on plate 1.

Distribution: The Bar-throated Apalis is found in well wooded or forested areas and has thus become quite common in many gardens. It occurs anywhere in Zimbabwe where suitable habitat is found.

Notes: The Bar-throated Apalis creeps about through the thick vegetation searching for insects and on the whole is rather inconspicuous until it starts to call, when the loud whistling notes immediately draw attention to the bird. It becomes very tame and will continue to move around quite close to an observer, thus allowing him to study it at leisure. The ball shaped nest is usually made of fine material covered with moss as a form of camouflage. Most of the nesting takes place during the early summer.

20 PARADISE FLYCATCHER (R.682)
Plate 5   *TERPSIPHONE VIRIDIS*

Field characters: The greenish blue head and crest and the russet plumage make this species very easy to identify in the field. The long tail feathers of the male are also very conspicuous at all times. The call is distinctive being a sharp 'Zwet-zwer'. This call may or may not be followed by a series of rippling whistles.

Distribution: The Paradise Flycatcher is found throughout Zimbabwe during the summer months, moving away in the winter. It is essentially a bird of the taller woodlands and has become well adapted to man's gardens. It is found in the vicinity of streams and is generally absent in the drier areas of Zimbabwe.

Notes: Because the bird has become so well known in gardens it is one of the species most noticed by those people who are not really interested in birds. They may build their beautiful little cup shaped nests within a few metres of houses where the young can be watched while the adults feed them. The males in particular spend a lot of time flying around the garden in a rather undulating flight, with the long tail feathers streaming out behind. They usually catch their prey by hawking from a perch, but may also pick insects off leaves or branches. Although the nest is usually placed in a fairly conspicuous position, because it is very well camouflaged with lichen it is difficult to spot, but once the chicks are being fed the frequent comings and goings of the parents soon draw attention to the nest.

21 BLUE-EARED GLOSSY STARLING (R.738)
Plate 25   *LAMPROTORNIS CHALYBAEUS*

Field characters: This starling is a wholly blue bird, but the blue does show a certain amount of variation in that the blue ear is fairly obvious when the bird is seen clearly. The call is probably the most important field character. This is a variety of whistles and warbles interspersed with a rather grating call which can be variously interpreted as 'Oh heck' or 'Squeare'. This is quite unlike the call of either the Lesser Blue-eared Glossy Starling whose call is 'Wiri-gwiri' and is in fact quite a musical note, or the Cape Glossy Starling which is a much darker bird, being almost indigo in colour, which again has a rather different call which may be rendered 'Turr-weeu'. In flight, the wings of Blue-eared Glossy Starlings are rather more rounded than those of the Lesser Glossy Starling and they do not creak as do the Cape Glossy Starlings' wings. The Blue-eared Glossy Starling usually occurs in pairs while outside the breeding season the Lesser Blue-eared Glossy Starling normally occurs in small to large flocks. The former may form flocks or join flocks of the latter as well.

Distribution: They are birds of the parkland savanna and have become attracted to the open lawns found around many of our Zimbabwean farmhouses. There they may be seen running around, with a noticeably upright stance, looking for insects. They are found throughout Zimbabwe apart from the driest areas, but nowhere are they particularly common.

Notes: The Blue-eared Glossy Starlings come to the bird table very readily to feed on mealie meal or fruit. They nest in holes and fence poles which are particularly favoured by this species. One pair at Peterhouse nested in the hollow concrete blocks used to build a castle for an open air play. When the battlements were dismantled the nest containing two chicks was found and the whole nest was transferred to a separate pile of concrete blocks where the adults successfully fledged their chicks. They will also nest under the eaves of houses and in any pipes which are available and they have therefore become well known to many Zimbabweans.

22 RED-WINGED STARLING (R.745)
Plate 32   *ONYCHOGNATHUS MORIO*

Field characters: The generally dark blue colour with the brick red 'windows' in the wings makes identification easy. The loud whistle 'Ti-juu' draws attention to the birds and they will answer you if you whistle at them.

Distribution: The Red-winged Starling may occur anywhere in Zimbabwe, but is only resident where there are rocky crags or cliffs, or in built up areas where buildings provide suitable nesting sites.

Notes: The Red-winged Starling has adapted well to the concrete jungle and is thus found in most towns and farms where there are nesting sites on the buildings. It often nests inside barns and other buildings. Unfortunately it is a very untidy bird which is thus not often welcome in dwelling houses. During the non-breeding season flocks of Red-winged Starlings may appear for a few days, feeding on insects and fruit such as wild figs before disappearing again, but pairs may remain near the nest throughout the year. Breeding takes place from September to February or March, early nestlings being fed large quantities of mulberries if available which results in the area below the nest being stained purple.

23 LESSER DOUBLE-COLLARED SUNBIRD (R.760)
Plate 1   *NECTARINIA CHALYBEUS*

Field characters: The long, thin, curved bill and very rapid flight distinguishes the sunbirds, and this species is easily recognised from other sunbirds by the green head and red breast. The female is a dull olive brown with a rather lighter belly and you should look at the size, thickness, and length of the bill for comparison with other sunbirds in order to identify the females. Most sunbirds occur in pairs and therefore it would be reasonable to assume that if a female sunbird were with a male Lesser Double-collared, then the female is the same species.

Distribution: The Lesser Double-collared Sunbird is essentially a bird of the brachystegia or miombo woodland, but also occurs in the mountainous parts of the Eastern Districts and westwards into Matabeleland wherever suitable woodland occurs.

Notes: In Mashonaland these are probably the best known of the sunbirds which occur in the gardens and they become extremely tame there. In the field they are very restless, moving rapidly from place to place in search of nectar or insects. They are readily attracted to tubular flowers such as Aloes and Salvia and they do much to enhance the beauty of the gardens. The nest appears to be built by the female, but the male is always in attendance and spends a considerable amount of time chasing the female as she moves back and forth gathering nest material. The nest may be built at any time of the year, but most of the nesting activity occurs during September and October. The nests I have found in the winter months have usually contained only one egg or chick whereas the summer nests normally contain two eggs or chicks. The long drawn out twittering call of the male is most noticeable during breeding.

24 SCARLET-CHESTED SUNBIRD (R.774)
Plate 3   *NECTARINIA SENEGALENSIS*

Field characters: Like most sunbirds of the genus *Nectarinia* the Scarlet-chested has a long curved bill which in this case is heavier than that of most of the other sunbirds in Zimbabwe. The male is easily identified because of his black plumage and brilliant scarlet chest. The throat, head, and shoulders may show some iridescence if the light is right. The female is a little more difficult to identify, but she is a rather heavily mottled bird and, as can be seen in the photograph on plate 3, the outer edges of the primaries and primary coverts are white which serve to distinguish her from the female Black Sunbird.

Distribution: The Scarlet-chested Sunbird occurs throughout Zimbabwe, but seems to move about depending on the availability of flowers. In some gardens where flowers are available throughout the year it would probably become resident.

Notes: Scarlet-chested Sunbirds are attracted to any flowers, but you probably notice them most often when the Erythirinias are in flower. Then they may be seen flitting around the flowers with a fairly rapid wing beat. During the early summer when they are breeding, the male calls continually from some vantage point in his territory. This call may be rendered as 'Tip-teeu-tip-tip'. The Scarlet-chested Sunbird has become very much adapted to man's settlement and often occurs as a nesting resident in gardens. Very often the preferred nesting site is on a creeper or bush growing up against the wall of a house, if possible under the eaves. The nests constructed under these circumstances do not deteriorate in winter and may therefore be used again the following year. If the same nest is not used, another nest may be built very close to the first one. One pair has successfully nested for three seasons on one of the boarding hostels at Peterhouse where the birds feeding their chicks have been watched by many boys. Feeding activities often go on even when boys are walking along the verandah near the nests.

25 YELLOW WHITE-EYE (R.777)
Plate 3   *ZOSTEROPS SENEGALENSIS*

Field characters: The Yellow White-eye is a small yellow bird with a very short sharp bill and a white ring around the eye which is usually very obvious in the field. The young birds lack this white ring and may therefore prove a little confusing. The rather high pitched whistling call is also of some use in identification and often draws attention to the birds.

Distribution: The Yellow White-eye may be found in any area of heavy woodland or forest throughout Zimbabwe, but in the drier western parts is probably restricted to riparian vegetation and gardens.

Notes: These are friendly little birds which move around in loose flocks keeping in contact with one another by a rather soft whistling 'Cheep-cheep'. They come very readily to bird tables where fruit is put out and also come to bathe at the bird bath. Unfortunately they are also very partial to soft fruits and therefore tend to be rather a pest when you are trying to grow peaches or other similar fruits. It should, however, be borne in mind that through most of the year they live largely on insects which would probably therefore destroy the fruit in the summer in any case. The nest is a beautiful little cup suspended near the end of a branch amongst the leaves. During the breeding season the white-eyes have a beautiful warbling song which is uttered from the top of a high tree. They are often seen searching for small insects among the leaves and then hopping or flying onto the next branch to repeat the process.

26 PIN-TAILED WHYDAH (R.846) *VIDUA MACROURA*
Plate 2

Field characters: During the summer the male with its distinctive black and white plumage and four long pin tail feathers is very easily identified, but in winter plumage the species is more difficult to distinguish from the other whydahs. It has a rather conical bill and the sides of the head are fairly heavily streaked as can be seen in the picture of the female shown on plate 2.

Distribution: The Pin-tailed Whydah may occur anywhere in Zimbabwe, normally in grassland areas with scattered trees or bushes. It is attracted to gardens where seed is put out on bird tables and may move into the garden during the breeding season if at no other time of the year.

Notes: The Pin-tailed Whydah parasitises the Common Waxbill and therefore you would normally expect to find it where there are Common Waxbills. I have found, however, that it often occurs where no Common Waxbills are to be seen and this raises the problem of where it lays its eggs. During the breeding season the males stake out a territory, which may well be your garden, and proceed to chase all seed eating birds, and in some cases other species as well, which enter their territory. They are particularly irritating at bird tables where they often discourage other species from feeding. Unfortunately it is almost impossible to eliminate them as their place is immediately taken by another male if the one in residence is trapped and removed. They have a form of courtship flight where the male hovers, with rapidly beating wings, in front of the female, the tail forming an undulating pattern as the bird moves up and down. Unlike most cuckoos, the whydahs do not eject the young of their hosts from the nests, but grow up amicably with them. They prefer to feed on the ground, but will feed quite readily at raised bird tables. In the Cape, I have seen one male terrorising the birds coming to bird tables set on a balcony on the first floor of a building.

27 YELLOW-EYED CANARY (R.859)
Plate 2   *SERINUS MOZAMBICUS*

Field characters: The Yellow-eyed Canary is another bird with a rather conical bill. The yellow eye stripe and rump on a generally greenish yellow background stand out and aid in its identification.

Distribution: It may occur in any woodland throughout Zimbabwe, but is probably most common in the brachystegia woodlands. It has moved into rural gardens in considerable numbers and has become very common particularly where seed is put out on bird tables.

Notes: Yellow-eyed Canaries often occur in small groups or flocks which feed on the ground, but shoot up to the top of the nearest tree at the slightest hint of danger. They are great singers and their pleasant warbling call may be heard at any time of the year although it is most prevalent during the early summer months. The nest, which may be built at any time of the year, is a shallow basin of fine material placed in a fork of a tree near the outer edge amongst the leaves.

28 STREAKY-HEADED SEED-EATER (R.867)
Plate 3   *SERINUS GULARIS*

Field characters: The Streaky-headed Seed-eater is a rather dull grey or greyish brown bird which often occurs in gardens and probably leads to some confusion of identity. The top of the head is noticeably streaked, but this is not always obvious in the field where the off-white lower parts and grey brown upper parts are the features most likely to be noticed.

Distribution: Once again this is a brachystegia bird which occurs very widely in Zimbabwe, although so far has not been recorded from the lowest lying parts of the country in the Zambezi and Limpopo Valleys.

Notes: Like the Yellow-eyed Canary it spends a lot of time singing from the tops of trees and is therefore popular in gardens. It comes to the bird table to feed but, like the Yellow-eyed Canary, flees at the first sign of danger. In flight it often spreads its wings so that they appear to be almost rounded and yet when it is flying normally the wings have a distinctively pointed appearance. In the hand this tapering of the primaries is very obvious.

Open water

The development of agriculture in Zimbabwe has resulted in the formation of a large number of bodies of open water which were not previously available. The building of dams and lakes obviously has supplemented the supply of natural pans and large pools on rivers, and probably has resulted in a fairly substantial increase in the birds which favour this environment. It is, however, noteworthy that in many cases the development of man-made dams does not supply suitable habitat for some species. Because dams need to be as deep as possible in relation to their surface area in order to reduce evaporation, the margins of the dams often slope sharply downwards or in the case of rocky areas the edges may drop precipitously into the water. This means that one does not have an area of relatively shallow water which is suitable for species such as herons to fish in. Nevertheless the smaller farm dams are usually excellent in that they slope quite gently down from the margin to the deepest point and in this respect they resemble natural pans. Natural pans are generally very shallow and this means they will probably dry up during the dry season which may tend to inhibit bird life to a certain extent. The areas of open water usually have a variety of distinctive habitats associated with them and each of these has its own characteristic bird fauna. In many cases this bird fauna is exactly the same as that of the rivers and one should therefore consider the two chapters on open water and rivers as being complementary and refer to both of them.

The dams and pans have the following habitats:

1   Open water where you may see species such as Cormorants and Darters fishing.

2   Areas of water lilies or polygonum where you would see Jacanas and Dabchicks.

3   Reed and sedge beds where Moorhens and Black Crakes hide.

4   Sandy or muddy margins with or without rocky outcrops where you would probably see the Treble-banded Sandplover.

All these different habitats are related to the water and all the species which occur are in fact attracted by the presence of water. In the case of those dams where water level does not fluctuate markedly, I think you will find that the last habitat, that of the sandy banks, becomes comparatively unimportant.

Reed beds are, to my way of thinking, the most frustrating habitat of all, in that they always have a variety of fascinating sounds coming from them, but it is quite impossible to see far enough into the reeds to identify the source. If you sit around for long enough, however, some birds will emerge from the reeds. Thus you may see the Black Crake creep out and walk around on the floating vegetation, feeding. Herons or other members of this family may fly up out of the reeds which often indicates that they are nesting within the reed beds. In the case of most of our reed beds, penetration is extremely difficult, not only because the reeds are extremely thick but also because the phragmites reeds have needle sharp tips to their leaves which makes passage through the reeds extremely uncomfortable.

The sedge beds or bullrush beds tend to attract birds such as the Red-knobbed Coot which builds its nest on the margins of the sedge. They are more often seen swimming around in the open water where their white shield immediately draws attention to themselves. In the sedge beds you are likely to see a variety of little brown warblers whose identification is extremely difficult unless you take the trouble to learn their calls. I have not, however, described any of these species in this volume.

29 DABCHICK (R.6) *TACHYBAPTUS RUFICOLLIS*
Plate 7

Field characters: The Dabchick is the smallest of the grebes in southern Africa and it is most likely to be seen swimming in the middle of a dam or pan. It is much smaller than any of the ducks, coots, or moorhens which are likely to be seen in similar circumstances and unlike most other birds which swim around on the water they dive at the first sign of danger. If seen clearly the rufous on the head and neck may be seen and it will be noted that the bill is not flat like that of a duck nor cylindrical like that of a moorhen. The light coloured skin at the gape is usually very obvious (see photograph on plate 7).

Distribution: The Dabchick may be found throughout Zimbabwe wherever suitable areas of open water occur and soon appears on pans and dams which have been filled up during the rains.

Notes: The Dabchick occurs in pairs or small groups usually near some form of aquatic vegetation but as far from the bank as possible. It swims fairly quickly across the water, but dives at the first sign of danger. If closely pursued it will rise from the water and with rapid wing beats fly along just above the surface, running across the surface of the water as it does so. The wings are comparatively small for the size of the bird. The Dabchick may also be seen to rise out of the water flapping its wings vigorously and shaking its body before settling back in very nearly the same place. It has a fairly loud trilling call which often draws attention to the Dabchick before it is actually seen. The nest is a floating one (see photograph on plate 7) which is anchored fairly securely to aquatic vegetation such as water lilies or polygonum, usually well out in the dam or pan. The Dabchick, like the other grebes, covers the eggs with nest material when it leaves the nest, thus the casual observer would believe that there were no eggs at all. The eggs soon become stained by the wet vegetation of which the nest is constructed. The young leave the nest immediately after hatching and in many instances have been recorded as riding on the backs of adult birds. On one occasion when I approached the nest of a Dabchick, the bird attempted to defend the nest by splashing me with water. The adult would swim towards me and then dive, somehow flipping water over me and the canoe. Unfortunately I could not see whether this water was splashed up by the wings or the feet of the diving bird, but suspect the latter.

30 REED CORMORANT (R.50)
Plate 8   *PHALACROCORAX AFRICANUS*

Field characters: The hooked bill readily distinguishes this from the Darter (see plate 8) and this, together with the rather long tail, serve to identify the Reed Cormorant. The bird itself is essentially a dark sooty brown, but the juveniles have a light, almost white breast.

Distribution: The Reed Cormorant may be found on any suitable dam or river throughout Zimbabwe where it is probably the most common cormorant.

Notes: When swimming, the Reed Cormorant practically disappears under the water because the feathers lack oil and therefore become waterlogged. Even here it is easily distinguished from the Darter because it has a comparatively thicker and shorter neck and the hooked bill should still be obvious. When they come out of the water both the Darter and the Reed Cormorant hang their wings out to dry. Reed Cormorants usually nest in colonies often in association with egrets and herons. They prefer to nest over water and the chicks dive overboard when danger threatens. Later they will swim back and clamber up the tree with much flapping of their partly developed wings in order to get back to the nest. In the non-breeding season they roost with Cattle Egrets in reed beds and may execute very complicated manoeuvres to lose altitude as they come in to roost.

31 DARTER (R.52)   *ANHINGA RUFA*
Plate 8

Field characters: The sharp pointed bill without a hook distinguishes the Darter from the cormorants. The long thin neck and long tail may be clearly seen in the field. The neck in particular is an important field character. The neck and upper breast are rufous in colour, but the rest of the bird is black with more or less white on the plumes on the back.

Distribution: The Darter occurs throughout Zimbabwe wherever suitable areas of open water occur and on some of the larger dams and pans it has become very common.

Notes: Like the cormorants, the Darter must dry its plumage after diving for fish and this is quite a common sight where they occur. In the water, only the head and neck is seen and the long thin neck has led to its common name of Snake Bird. The Darters are also colonial nesters and are often found with cormorants and egrets.

32 GREY HERON (R.54) *ARDEA CINEREA*
Plate 12

Field characters: All herons have long sharply pointed bills and usually they have very long slender necks. In flight this neck is carried folded (this is shown in the illustration) and this serves to distinguish herons from storks which fly with their necks stretched out in front of them. The Grey Heron is a much lighter bird than the Black-headed Heron and lacks the black crown and neck of this species. The neck, as can be seen in the photograph on plate 12, is white. The white eyebrow is also a good field characteristic.

Distribution: The Grey Heron may occur anywhere in Zimbabwe, but is probably nowhere very common. It prefers the larger dams and rivers, but may occur on any open water.

Notes: The Grey Heron is usually seen sitting on a dead stump or tree unless it is fishing, when it either stands motionless in the water or walks very slowly along the edge of the reeds or other vegetation in the dam. Food is captured by a sharp stabbing motion of the head and neck. Unlike the Black-headed Heron, the Grey Heron is a solitary bird and does not normally join up with other herons. The Grey Heron nests in the company of the other herons, but usually the nest is placed on the edge of the colony possibly some distance away from the other birds. Sometimes the Grey Heron is found some distance from water and may be seen feeding in grassland, particularly after rain or when the ground is rather damp or marshy. It is probably attracted to these areas by the frogs which occur in numbers under these conditions.

33 KNOB-BILLED DUCK (R.91)
Plate 8 *SARKIDIORNIS MELANOTOS*

Field characters: The dark almost black back and wings contrast strongly with the white lower neck and belly. In flight the wings have a blue green colour which shows up very clearly in some lights. The knob on the male's bill varies in size, becoming larger during the breeding season.

Distribution: The Knob-billed Duck is found throughout Zimbabwe and may turn up on any body of water. It has become

47   Senegal Coucal
15″/375 mm   *Peter Ginn*

44   Black Crake
9″/225 mm   *Bill Nichol*

Plate 9

45   Blacksmith Plover
11″/275 mm   *Peter Ginn*

46   Wood Sandpiper
8″/200 mm   *Eliot Lyons*

39   Three-banded Sandplover   7″/175 mm   *Cyril Laubscher*

Plate 10

62   Crowned Plover   12″/300 mm   *Cyril Laubscher*

53   Wattled Plover   13″/325 mm   *Peter Ginn*

1   Red-eyed Dove
13″/325 mm   *Peter Ginn*

4   Red-faced Mousebird
13″/325 mm   *Peter Ginn*

Plate 11

74   Carmine Bee-eater
14″/350 mm   *Peter Ginn*

75   Lilac-breasted Roller
14″/350 mm   *Ray Cock*

32 Grey Heron
40″/1 000 mm   *Ray Cock*

68 White Stork
46″/1 150 mm   *Peter Ginn*

Plate 12

69 Secretary Bird
50″/1 250 mm   *Bill Nichol*

60 Abdim's Stork
30″/750 mm   *Peter Ginn*

8   Fiscal Shrike   9″/225 mm   *Peter Ginn*

7   Heuglin's Robin   8″/200 mm   *Peter Ginn*

Plate 13

65   Buffy Pipit   7½″/187 mm   *Peter Ginn*

57   Red-collared Widow Bird ♂ Br   57   Red-collared Widow Bird ♀
16″/400 mm   *Cyril Laubscher*   5″/125 mm   *Peter Ginn*

Plate 14

99   Golden-breasted Bunting   11   House Sparrow ♂
105 Violet-eared Waxbill ♂ *B. Nichol*   5½″/140 mm   *Peter Ginn*

54 Stonechat ♂
5½"/140 mm   *Bill Nichol*

54 Stonechat ♀
5½"/140 mm   *Cyril Laubscher*

Plate 15

63 Rufous-naped Lark
7"/175 mm   *Peter Ginn*

64 Rattling Cisticola
6"/150 mm   *Peter Ginn*

76   Masked Weaver ♂ Br
6″/150 mm   *Bill Nichol*

76   Masked Weaver ♀
5½″/140 mm   *Peter Ginn*

Plate 16

66   Red-billed Quelea ♀
5″/125 mm   *Peter Ginn*

56   Red Bishop Bird ♂ Br
5″/125 mm   *Bill Nichol*

a regular rooster at Ballantyne Park in Harare where it can be studied very easily. It probably exhibits considerable movement around the country.

Notes: This duck may build up to large numbers at certain times of the year on favoured bodies of water particularly those bodies used for roosting. The parties coming in to roost execute some remarkable movements as they spill air from their wings in order to lose altitude, and then use their wings to brake their descent.

34 RED-BILLED TEAL (R.97)
Plate 17   *ANAS ERYTHRORHYNCHA*

Field characters: The division of the head into a dark crown and light cheek is usually fairly obvious in the field and a good view will reveal the red bill. In flight the fairly fast wing beat is typical of most of our ducks, but the speculum (the coloured window in the wing) is a light chestnut colour with a narrow dark brown line near the leading edge.

Distribution: Probably the most common of the ducks in Zimbabwe, this species may occur on any dam or pan.

Notes: The Red-billed Teal appears to be migratory—certainly large concentrations appear to build up during the summer months in Zimbabwe and numbers decrease during the winter. When feeding, although it may up-end, it generally tends to feed by merely dipping the bill under the water. When breeding the Red-billed Teal will feign injury to a wing if one approaches the nest or ducklings. The bird appears to have a broken wing and be unable to fly and it flutters off across the ground dragging the wing behind it. If you follow the bird it will lead you some distance from the nest and then suddenly take off and fly away quite normally.

35 FISH EAGLE (R.149)   *HALIAEETUS VOCIFER*
Plate 18

Field characters: Like all eagles it has a large hooked bill and heavy talons. The white head with a dark back and rufous shoulders and belly readily distinguish this eagle in the field. The ringing call, uttered with a marked throwing back of the head, is one of the best known sounds of Africa and may be heard throughout the continent from Ethiopia southwards.

Distribution: Although found throughout Zimbabwe it is generally more common at lower levels, but may be resident on any suitable large river or dam. It does visit the smaller dams or rivers with large pools for short periods but is not resident there.

Notes: To me this is one of the typical birds of the wilds of Africa and fortunately it is protected by most people and so is still relatively common. It feeds on any dead fish that it may find and sometimes catches its own fish by swooping into the water when the fish is near the surface. It also eats other aquatic animals such as frogs and toads if it can catch them. I have seen it feeding on toads mating in the shallow water of the Botletle River in Botswana as these were readily available. The nest is typical of the larger eagles in that it is a large platform of sticks placed high up in a tree near the water. When the eggs are laid the nest is lined with a few sprays of green leaves.

36 MOORHEN (R.210)   *GALLINULA CHLOROPUS*
Plate 6

Field characters: The Moorhen is generally blue black all over except for the white on the wings and under-tail coverts. Above the bill is a red shield which is not always very obvious.

Distribution: It may occur anywhere in Zimbabwe where there is suitable open water with reeds to which the bird can retreat.

Notes: If you are prepared to sit quietly on a stretch of water where reeds and reed beds occur the chances are that sooner or later a moorhen will emerge and swim around looking for food. While it does this it often cocks its tail up exposing the white undertail coverts and, if danger threatens, this tail cocking becomes most marked, the white probably acting as a danger signal to other members of the species. It then retreats rapidly into the reeds from where it may be heard calling. At times it is quite noisy and thus can be rather frustrating as the calls come from the depths of the reed beds. Unlike the Lesser Moorhen, the Moorhen is not so prone to hiding in the reeds and will come out into the open water to feed where you may then study it.

37 RED-KNOBBED COOT (R.212) *FULICA CRISTATA*
Plate 6

Field characters: Although similar in colour to the Moorhen, the coot has a white shield and it lacks the white on wings and tail. It is also usually more obvious in that it spends more time out in the open areas. The red knobs on the top of the head become enlarged during the breeding season, but are otherwise not easy to see.

Distribution: Once again, the Red-knobbed Coot occurs throughout Zimbabwe, but on the whole it will be found only on larger bodies of water that accommodate the Moorhen. It also seems to prefer the shorter sedge beds rather than the tall bullrush and reed beds favoured by the Moorhen. Breeding takes place within or on the margins of the sedge beds.

Notes: Pairs of coots can usually be found in most suitable areas but in favoured locations it may gather in very large numbers indeed. Where numbers of birds gather there is usually quite a lot of movement with birds chasing one another over the water. This chasing is usually accompanied by a skittering or a running over the water with the wings flapping noisily. The bird will also do this if pursued closely. The coot is very much less secretive than the Moorhen and so is quite often seen where they occur. The call, a rather distinctive coughing sound, is characteristic.

38 AFRICAN JACANA (R.228)
Plate 6   *ACTOPHILORNIS AFRICANUS*

Field characters: The Jacana is a bird which is probably most easily identified by its habit of walking across the floating vegetation in search of insects. The tremendously long toes enable the foot to cover a large area and thus the bird is able to walk on the minimum of floating material. Nevertheless, it is a striking bird with its russet body, white neck, and blue shield and if clearly seen the colours also help to identify it. In flight the rather rounded wings and long toes trailing out behind the bird are also characteristic.

Distribution: The Jacana is restricted to areas with sufficient floating vegetation for it to find food, where it is often common.

Notes: The birds move very rapidly over floating vegetation and yet do not hesitate to fly if alarmed. They will also swim on occasions particularly if attacked by some bird of prey or when they need to get their chicks across open water. The birds nest on a pad of floating material, old Dabchicks' nests for example, which have grasses or other vegetation growing on them. The three eggs are laid in a slight depression in the top of the pad and are some of the most beautiful eggs in the country. They are pyriform in shape and are a mustard colour covered with scrolls, lines, and dots of black. They have a remarkably high gloss as though they have been polished. The Jacanas are noisy birds and may be heard calling at any time during the day although at times their call appears to have a rather ventriloquial quality and it is difficult to decide just what is calling.

39 TREBLE-BANDED SANDPLOVER (R.238)
Plate 10   *CHARADRIUS TRICOLLARIS*

Field characters: The Treble-banded Sandplover is a fairly small plover-like bird which spends much of its time walking along the edge of the water searching for insects. The two black bars across the breast separated by a white line and the red ring around the eye are useful field characters if the bird is clearly seen. Unfortunately the birds often tend to run away from you thus obscuring the bars on the breast.

Distribution: This bird occurs throughout Zimbabwe, but is probably a more common resident on the plateau than at lower levels. On the plateau it occurs on even the smallest dams provided there is a muddy margin where it can find insects.

Notes: The Treble-banded Sandplover usually occurs in pairs although on occasions it may gather in quite large numbers if flooding of open ground has occurred. The bird has a bobbing action which normally occurs with each call, but which also occurs when the bird stops running. The call is a rather high pitched whistle which could be rendered 'Tiuu-it, tiuu-it'. The nest is a shallow depression usually lined with a few pebbles or bits of mud. The eggs are cryptically coloured and are therefore rather difficult to spot.

River and riparian fringe

The rivers in Zimbabwe are very varied and it is impossible to describe in detail anything like all the possible habitats one may find along them. The plateau has many small streams flowing in fairly steepsided valleys with numerous rapids and small waterfalls. The rapids are normally separated by small to large pools or at least stretches of relatively gentle flow with reed beds or rank grass. The banks may or may not be lined with denser vegetation than the surrounding areas, but often there is no marked change in the vegetation as one approaches the river. As you descend from the plateau the streams coalesce to form ever larger rivers which may have large sandbanks covered only during floods. Here you may see the Egyptian Goose standing on the sand during the day. The reed beds tend to become larger and denser and the banks may have marked gallery forests with dense undergrowth. In the lower lying areas the large rivers normally have gallery forests and within these you may find very dense undergrowth, a lot of it quite impenetratable, and it is here that you will find species which do not occur elsewhere.

The rivers, particularly the larger ones, are obviously a major source of water, but this does not become markedly noticeable until one penetrates the lower lying areas or areas where it is relatively dry. The development of the gallery forest results in the growth of very large trees along the river banks, often with species which are not found in the surrounding woodlands. As one moves away from the river so the height and density of the forest decreases until it passes gradually into the vegetation of the surrounding areas. The development of undergrowth is usually also encouraged although I have found in some places that the undergrowth has largely disappeared because of extensive grazing. The gallery forest is therefore something which is rather atypical of the area and it is here that one finds certain species which will not occur in the surrounding countryside. The vegetation within the gallery forest is for the most part similar

to that of the surrounding woodlands and therefore if you find
hornbills for example in the area, they will probably also occur
along the river.

The common denominator of rivers is the presence of water
and this in turn leads to the presence of certain species which
would not otherwise occur. For example you will find the
Blacksmith Plover occurring along the rivers, particularly where
there are suitable sandbanks, while the Crowned Plover will
occur in the surrounding areas which are open enough for it.
The Blacksmith Plover is always associated with water although
it may move away from it during certain seasons of the year,
whereas the Crowned Plover is a dry land plover associated with
short grass or open areas. The waders such as Wood Sandpipers
are also attracted to water and may be seen feeding along the
margins of both rivers and dams.

In the case of rivers, dams or other areas of water, you have the
great advantage of being able to sit and watch the birds coming
down to drink, and in this way you can learn a great deal about
the species which inhabit the surrounding areas. In the wetter
areas this is probably not so profitable but in the drier west and
the lowveld one sees a continual stream of birds coming down to
drink. The river is perhaps a little more difficult as there is water
over a long distance, but if you walk along the river you will
soon realise that the birds have favourite drinking spots, usually
where there is a tree near an open area of water, to which they
come in large numbers. If you station yourself at one of these
drinking places you are likely to see a very much greater variety
of species than you would by merely walking around. The
species which will appear are determined to a large extent by the
habitats in the surrounding areas.

40 HAMERKOP (R.72)   *SCOPUS UMBRETTA*
Plate 4

Field characters: The Hamerkop is readily identified in the
field by its hammer shaped head, but you should remember that
the crest of feathers at the back of the head can be laid down
against the neck. It is a plain brown bird and in this respect it
does not resemble any other species which may occur in the same
habitat.

Distribution: It is found throughout Zimbabwe wherever suitable pools, pans and rivers occur.

Notes: Hamerkops live essentially on frogs and other aquatic animals and are therefore usually seen stalking along the edges of dams or pans in shallow water searching for prey. They usually hunt with the crest up; in flight the bill is pointed forward and the crest therefore lies flat against the neck, but still it can be seen as a noticeable bump. Hamerkops build very interesting and unique nests of sticks plastered together with mud. These huge domed nests are built by both birds over a period of several weeks and are extremely strong, a nest lasting for many years.

Unfortunately the nests are also favoured by Barn Owls and these will evict the rightful owners if opportunity offers. Other birds such as Egyptian Geese have been known to nest on top of a Hamerkop's nest or inside the nest chamber once the roof has fallen in. The nest is usually placed in a fork of a tree or on a ledge on a cliff. The entrance is placed on the underside facing the overhang and is therefore very difficult to reach.

41 EGYPTIAN GOOSE (R.89)
Plate 8   *ALOPOCHEN AEGYPTIACUS*

Field characters: The Egyptian Goose has a slower wing beat than the ducks' and is much larger than all but the Knob-billed Duck. It is usually first noticed by its hoarse honking call as it flies along. The bird is generally a reddish brown colour with white on the wings which is very obvious in flight and can be seen even when the bird is at rest. If a good frontal view is obtained the brown patch on the breast is quite distinctive.

Distribution: It occurs throughout Zimbabwe, but is probably more common on the larger rivers where there are suitable sandbanks on which it likes to rest. It is relatively uncommon over much of the plateau although it does turn up on dams from time to time.

Notes: Normally Egyptian Geese occur in pairs, but where suitable habitat occurs they may gather in large numbers. On one visit to Aisleby farm near Bulawayo I was able to watch nearly 200 geese resting on the grass slopes near the dam. The Egyptian Goose will nest almost anywhere such as on the top of the old nests of Hamerkops or birds of prey, in holes in trees, and so on. One pair has even been known to rear its goslings successfully in the steeple of the cathedral in Grahamstown. When the goslings are very young they dive at the first sign of danger, but when they first reach the water they do not seem to be able to dive properly, merely putting their heads under and beating the air with their feet. This is something which would make a very amusing cine film if it could be caught. Egyptian Geese feed at night and are therefore usually seen during the day sitting on sandbanks or other suitable open ground. They often feed in farm lands, where they can do considerable damage to young plants.

42 WHITE-FACED DUCK (R.100)
Plate 17   *VIDUATA DENDROCYGNA*

Field characters: The loud whistling call of this duck is a very important field character, as is the white face.

Distribution: Once again this bird occurs throughout Zimbabwe, but is much more common in the lower lying areas. It may reach large numbers during the wet season in Matabeleland and probably appears in any numbers on the plateau only during this period. It usually favours open rivers with mudbanks.

Notes: The White-faced Duck is normally encountered in quite large flocks which take off and wheel around when disturbed. In flight the dark wings and rump are obvious. They are nocturnal feeders and are therefore usually seen during the day resting on mudbanks or sandbanks near water. The tri-syllabic call is a very clear whistle which is rendered 'Mai-wi-wi', usually uttered as the bird flies overhead or comes in to land.

43 SWAINSON'S FRANCOLIN (R.185)
Plate 31   *FRANCOLINUS SWAINSONII*

Field characters: All francolins are very fast runners and Swainson's Francolin is no exception. It is a dark bird with a red neck and eye. The outline is typical of francolins.

Distribution: Swainson's Francolin occurs over much of Zimbabwe although it appears to be missing in parts of the Eastern Districts, where its place is taken by the Red-necked Francolin.

Notes: Where the Swainson's and Red-necked Francolin occur together, such as between Marondera and Headlands, they sometimes interbreed and a number of hybrids have been collected. Swainson's Francolin seems to be rather local, although widespread, and will not necessarily occur throughout an area. They will usually be found near water where there is suitable cover to which they can retreat. They may cause considerable havoc in newly planted grain lands and are therefore often shot by farmers, although in fact this may be an excuse for they make excellent eating. The male usually finds a prominent calling post on the top of a rock or ant-heap and crows from there in early morning and in late evening with a rather harsh repetitious call. It is this calling which very often draws attention to the presence of Swainson's Francolin in an area where it is not otherwise seen.

44 BLACK CRAKE (R.203)
Plate 9   *LIMNOCORAX FLAVIROSTRA*

Field characters: This is a wholly black bird with a conspicuous greenish bill and rather dull red legs. Like all crakes it cocks its tail in the air while moving around.

Distribution: The Black Crake occurs throughout Zimbabwe wherever suitable habitat is found. It favours rivers and dams where there are extensive reed and bullrush beds with areas of floating vegetation along their margins.

Notes: The Black Crake is quite a common bird in Zimbabwe, but it is not seen unless you are prepared to sit quietly near a suitable body of water and wait for it to come out of the reeds. It is not nearly as secretive as the other crakes and spends a lot of time feeding near the margins of reed beds to which it rapidly retreats at the first sign of danger. This is another one of those irritating birds which insist on calling from the middle of the reeds and which can nearly drive you mad trying to find out what they are. However, if you have a tape recorder and can record the call, it is quite easy, by playing back the call, to get them to come out into the open where you can see them. As can be seen from the photograph on plate 9 the nest is a deep basin of bullrushes, or other water plants, stuck in the middle of the bullrushes, just above the water level.

45 BLACKSMITH PLOVER (R.245)
Plate 9   *VANELLUS ARMATUS*

Field characters: The high pitched ringing call (like the sound of two pieces of metal being struck together) from which it gets its name is characteristic and usually draws attention to the bird. The black and white plumage is also outstanding and characteristic.

Distribution: The Blacksmith Plover is found throughout Zimbabwe where suitable habitat occurs, but is generally rather rare on the higher parts of the plateau. It occurs on rivers and also dams and pans. It needs areas of open mud or sand.

Notes: If you are walking along a river the Blacksmith Plovers will spend considerable time flying over your head calling continuously. Despite the striking black and white plumage it is interesting to see how a Blacksmith Plover sitting on the ground can disappear into the background showing that black and white can be a cryptic colouring. Blacksmith Plovers usually occur in pairs, but at certain times of the year may gather in huge flocks in suitable locations. They prefer damper conditions than the Crowned Plover, although on some occasions will occur alongside the latter. They do not hesitate to dive-bomb you if you approach the nest or chicks, but they do not seem to press home the attack to quite the same degree that the Crowned Plover does. The bird lays three or four cryptically coloured eggs in a hollow in the ground which is usually lined with a few bits of mud or small pebbles. The birds are territorial and the male spends much of his time defending his territory against intruders.

46 WOOD SANDPIPER (R.264) *TRINGA GLAREOLA*
Plate 9

Field characters: The sandpipers are usually seen working their way along the edge of water bodies or across marshes and the Wood Sandpiper is no exception to this. This medium sized sandpiper is probably best identified by its characteristic call, a clear whistling 'Chiff-iff-iff' which is usually uttered as the bird takes off. The white rump is also obvious when the bird is in flight, and on the ground the spotted back, light eye-stripe, and fairly long bill are features which help to identify the Wood Sandpiper.

Distribution: The Wood Sandpiper is found throughout Zimbabwe, being limited only by the presence of suitable habitat.

Notes: The Wood Sandpiper is a bird of the mudbanks, but will also move into overgrown marshes to feed. It is quite often put up in areas where there is almost continuous grass cover, provided the whole area is muddy. The Wood Sandpiper is essentially a solitary bird, but flocks of variable size may gather where suitable food supplies occur. They are palaearctic migrants—migrants which breed in the Arctic Tundra of northern Eurasia—which leave Zimbabwe in early May and return in late August. Some birds stay throughout the winter. It is interesting that, in the case of the migrants, those birds which breed furthest north are the last to leave and the first to return to Zimbabwe. This is because their nesting grounds on the Tundra are the last part to warm up and become habitable. The Wood Sandpiper is usually seen hunting the flooded areas or mud for insects or small molluscs, but it generally does not probe the mud as much as some of the other waders do. In flight they are very fast and erratic, usually flying quite low and suddenly alighting on the ground, whereupon the head is bobbed once or twice.

47 SENEGAL or FLECK'S COUCAL (R.355)
Plate 9 *CENTROPUS SENEGALENSIS*

Field characters: The coucals are all fairly similar in general appearance, in that they have a heavy bill, rather elongated body with a long, heavy tail, and in flight the whole appearance is one of laboured movement. They therefore often glide along. The Fleck's Coucal has a reddish brown back as do many of the others, but this species has a plain rump which contrasts with the barred rump of other species which look similar.

Distribution: This coucal occurs over most of Zimbabwe where suitable thick cover occurs. The choice of habitat usually means that this bird is found in association with rivers, but it may occur almost anywhere and if suitable cover is present it may be found a long way from water.

Notes: The coucals are noisy birds and the tooting calls of the Fleck's Coucal can often be heard coming from the middle of a dense patch of bush. The bird is not often seen unless it flies from one patch of bush to the next, but is very fond of sunbathing and on a cool morning may be seen sitting on the top of a bush where it can catch the first sun. If disturbed, it soon disappears into the thick bush. The nest is an interesting one, in that it is a dome shaped nest which is made so roughly and untidily that it looks disused and old even when recently constructed.

48 PIED KINGFISHER (R.394) *CERYLE RUDIS*
Plate 6

Field characters: The Pied Kingfisher has the typical long, straight kingfisher bill and with its striking black and white plumage it is a relatively easy bird to identify. The habits are also useful field characters (see below). The male has two chest bars, and the female one (see photograph on plate 6).

Distribution: The Pied Kingfisher is another species which may occur anywhere in Zimbabwe where suitable habitat is found, but in general it seems to be less common on the higher parts of the plateau and the Eastern Districts. Because it prefers areas of open water it is seldom found along tree shaded rivers.

Notes: Pied Kingfishers always seem to seek out prominent perches over water from which they can watch below for fish. They have found that telephone lines or bridges crossing rivers form excellent perches. When sitting on a perch they bend the head forward, pointing the bill towards the water, and they may dive straight from the perch onto a fish below. Another common form of hunting is for the Pied Kingfishers to fly up and down across the water until they spot a fish, when they hover with the body forward and close their wings to plummet into the water with a splash. If the fish is small it is eaten immediately, but larger fish are carried to a perch where they are beaten and then turned round and swallowed head first. Pied Kingfishers are noisy birds and when they are in parties periodically chatter in unison. This is particularly noticeable if another kingfisher joins a pair or a party of kingfishers. They nest in holes in a bank, preferably over water, and it is noticeable that the nest becomes infested with small mites once there are chicks present.

49 MALACHITE KINGFISHER (R.397)
Plate 7   *ALCEDO CRISTATA*

Field characters: The Malachite Kingfisher is one of the three small kingfishers in Zimbabwe and it is readily distinguished from the other two in that it has a bright red bill and a greenish blue crest which extends down to the eye. It is usually found along waterways, whereas the Natal Kingfisher, which is very similar, is normally found in woodland.

Distribution: This species can occur anywhere in Zimbabwe although on the whole it is less common in the higher parts. I have found that it is often quite local in occurrence and can always be found along a particular stretch of river but absent from the areas on either side. This may well be tied up with a control related to the habitat.

Notes: If you are lucky enough to see the Malachite Kingfisher before it flies, you will probably see it sitting on a perch low down near the water and often under some overhanging vegetation. The birds sit there watching the water and dive from the perch onto small fish or other prey below. They usually allow a fairly close approach and you are able to study them carefully.

Once the bird takes off it flashes away at high speed just above the water and then will land on a branch some distance up the river. In flight the blue back and wings and the red beak are usually obvious and this bird is perhaps one of our most beautiful. The nest, like that of the Pied Kingfisher, is in a bank over water and once again the nest becomes rather smelly and infested with mites when the chicks are older. When the bird comes out of the nest it usually dives into the water near the nest in order to clear itself of the mites picked up in the nest. This process may be repeated a number of times each time the adult emerges.

50 PIED WAGTAIL (R.684) *MOTACILLA AGUIMP*

Field characters: The striking black and white pattern coupled with the slow walk and wagging tail make the Pied Wagtail easy to identify. In association with man it becomes very tame and therefore is easy to study.

Distribution: This bird is found throughout Zimbabwe especially along rivers where there are sandbanks or at least bare banks with little or no vegetation. It is often found on larger dams and, where these have been developed for recreation, Pied Wagtails have become permanent residents on grassy areas near boat clubs, game camps, and so on.

Notes: Pied Wagtails are confiding birds which will move into gardens if these are suitable, but here they may suffer from the effects of pesticides applied to the plants. In at least one case I know of, the Pied Wagtails were completely eliminated by the development of large scale spraying to control grass pests. They are usually associated with water and seem to be particularly fond of those rivers which have boulders exposed in the middle of the water. At the same time they like open water and are therefore not normally found along streams which are well shaded by thick bush or trees. In this habitat their place may well be taken by the Long-tailed Wagtail. When feeding, they stalk along with the tail usually held quite still or possibly wagging slowly until some insect is seen. The bird rushes forward to grab the insect or food and when it stops running, the tail is wagged rapidly three or four times. The wagtails build a deep cup shaped nest, usually in a bank or in flood debris fairly close to the water. In a number of instances I have found their nests flooded by water rising in a dam.

Vlei and rank grass

The development of vleis is to a large extent determined by the presence of fairly flat areas with some form of impervious layer just below the surface. Where they occur you normally find that the vegetation is markedly different from the surrounding areas in that there are relatively few trees while the grasses tend to become very much taller than those of the surrounding areas. Most vleis are of a temporary nature merely occurring during the rainy season, but there are permanent vleis which are normally associated with sponges which are fed by water from underground sources. The sponge is really a spring which has become completely overgrown so that the water outlet is not visible.

Permanent vleis with their associated sedge beds will attract species such as the Crowned Crane and the Marsh Harrier. These birds need fairly large areas of moist ground to be able to nest successfully. Less permanent vleis will usually be populated by species such as the Stonechat and Yellow-throated Longclaw. These birds like areas of fairly thick rank grass and can be found there throughout the year even if the ground becomes fairly dry during the dry season. The Red Bishop Birds move into wet areas during the rains to breed, but during the dry season they are usually found in grassland areas in association with widow birds or queleas.

Once again, man has, in some cases, caused the development of vleis. The upper end of some dams becomes a vlei during the rainy season, or, where drains run out into a comparatively flat area, this may result in the development of a fairly obvious vlei. Here again, unless you are prepared to don gum boots and walk through the wet areas, you will find that the vlei areas are rather irritating in that one can hear the birds, but very often cannot see them.

51 MARSH HARRIER (R.167) *CIRCUS AERUGINOSUS*
Plate 31

Field characters: The Marsh Harrier is probably most easily identified by its habit of flying with a rather slow heavy beat across marshy areas as it quarters the ground in search of prey. The reddish brown chest and thighs (see photograph on plate 31) are usually obvious if the bird is clearly seen, and the lighter shoulder patches stand out as the bird banks and corners. The wings are long and do not appear to taper very much, and the tail is also comparatively long.

Distribution: The Marsh Harrier is widespread and common in Mashonaland, but because of the decrease in suitable habitat as you move westwards it becomes less and less common the further west you go. If suitable habitat occurs, however, the bird may be found anywhere in Zimbabwe.

Notes: The Marsh Harrier is essentially a marshland hunter, but it will also move out over adjoining grassland or cultivated lands in search of prey. Unless disturbed or courting it seldom rises far above the ground, merely gliding and flying some 3 to 4 metres above the top of the grass. When it spots prey it executes a sudden turn and drops down into the grass; this movement has been described as looking as though the bird were shot. The nest is built inside sedge or reeds in marshy areas often over standing water. The bird flies low over the reeds as it approaches the nest and then drops very suddenly into it. This gives a rough landing, so much so that in the nest at which the photograph was taken the bird knocked the chick out on one occasion.

52 CROWNED CRANE (R.214)
Plate 4   *BALEARICA REGULORUM*

Field characters: The Crowned Cranes, like the other species of crane in southern Africa, are large birds with long necks and legs. This crane is very obvious even in silhouette and it is probably the crest which is first noticed. The white cheeks and wings are very striking and are noticeable if the light is right. The russet tail is also usually visible.

Distribution: Once again this species is limited by the availability of habitat, but is found fairly often on the plateau wherever there are large vleis.

Notes: Crowned Cranes are generally fairly tame birds unless they have been harassed. They have suffered due to the destruction of the swamps in which they normally occur and are probably not as common as formerly. They nest in the middle of swampy areas, nesting being preceded by an elaborate courtship ritual with the birds dancing and bowing to one another. The trumpeting call which may be rendered as 'Mayhem' has given rise to its Afrikaans name. During the breeding season they also have a fairly deep booming call. Breeding normally takes place during the rains, once vleis have filled up and the sedges have grown to a reasonable height.

53 WATTLED PLOVER (R.247)
Plate 10   *VANELLUS SENEGALLUS*

Field characters: The Wattled Plover usually draws attention to itself by its rather harsh noisy call and this is undoubtedly the best single field character once you have learnt it. The call is uttered both on the ground and while the bird is in flight. It grows in intensity as you approach the bird. When seen, the wattles and brown and white plumage are distinctive and this species should cause no problems with identification.

Distribution: The Wattled Plover is usually found near water or on the margins of vleis and is a common resident on the plateau. In the lower lying parts of Zimbabwe its place is largely taken by the White-crowned Plover. The Wattled Plover likes fairly open ground with short grass and is likely to occur where these features are near a river or water.

Notes: Wattled Plovers are very noisy birds which are found either in pairs or in small parties. They keep in touch with one another with a rather muted 'Zip' or 'Kip'. They favour wet marshy ground for feeding, but may move quite some distance from water at times, and if fields are irrigated will also move in here to feed. They are courageous birds and will not hesitate to defend their nests against intruders. While I was photographing the bird shown on plate 10, a herd of cows came over to investigate the hide. This of course brought them into the vicinity of the nest, over which the bird stood screaming at the cows, and in this way was able to keep them away from the eggs. The wings were held out and the bird stretched to its maximum height during this threat display. Dogs are dive-bombed and the bird may almost strike the dog. The birds defend the whole piece of territory they have staked out for their nesting activities, but the intensity of their attack is increased as one approaches the nest. The eggs are superbly camouflaged being merely laid in a slight hollow in the ground. Nesting usually takes place in the early summer and the chicks leave the nest as soon as they hatch.

54 STONECHAT (R.576)   *SAXICOLA TORQUATA*
Plate 15

Field characters: The male with its black and white plumage is easily identified, but the plain coloured female is perhaps not as easy although the white shoulders and rump are usually obvious. The habit of sitting on a prominent perch in grassland from which it either hawks or pounces on insects is a good guide to identification. Like all the chats it flicks its wings downwards on alighting, but does it less often than some other species.

Distribution: Apart from the Zambezi Valley, it is widespread and common wherever suitable moist grassland habitat occurs. It is essentially a bird of the moister grasslands, usually occurring on the margins of vleis and marshes. It may, however, also be found in drier grasslands and has even adapted to cultivated areas where the crops are not too tall nor too dense.

Notes: The Stonechat likes to sit on a tall grass stem or other prominent perch from which it can scan the surrounding area for insects. It calls frequently from the perch and the alarm call often draws attention to the bird before you notice it sitting there. The nest is a very neat cup placed under overhanging grass, often at the end of a sort of tunnel through the grass. When you approach the nest the bird becomes very agitated and will flit from perch to perch uttering a sort of buzzing 'Tsik-tsik' which carries remarkably well. It has become quite tame where it occurs in association with man.

55 YELLOW-THROATED LONGCLAW (R.704)
Plate 7   *MACRONYX CROCEUS*

Field characters: This is the largest of our longclaws and in flight appears to be very much heavier than the other species in Zimbabwe. The throat is yellow which contrasts with the orange of the Orange-throated Longclaw and the pink of the Pink-throated Longclaw, but as the bird tends to turn away from one this is often an unsatisfactory field character. The back is very much darker than that of the Orange-throated Longclaw and the pattern is generally more distinct. The gorget or bib is also very much more marked than is the case in the other longclaws. If the feet are seen the long hind claw is obvious, but generally these birds are in grassland and the feet probably will not be seen.

Distribution: The Yellow-throated Longclaw occurs over much of the eastern half of Zimbabwe, but it is limited by the presence of suitable marshland habitat. It seems to prefer rather longer, denser grass than the Orange-throated Longclaw.

Notes: All longclaws like a habitat similar to that of the vlei grasslands. You may find them all together and certainly in the Marandellas area all three species have been recorded at the same piece of vlei. The Orange-throated Longclaw favours shorter, lighter grassy areas to the other two species and the Pink-throated Longclaw seems to be very localised in habitat. The calls of all three species are similar and yet different, and if heard clearly they can be used to differentiate the species. The nest is placed under overhanging grass in a moist area and is usually very difficult to find. The bird shown in the photograph on plate 7 was ringed and has been retrapped over a period of three years, despite the fact that it is completely lame in the right leg. This bird had a most peculiar rolling gait as a result of this lameness.

56 RED BISHOP BIRD (R.808)   *EUPLECTES ORIX*
Plate 16

Field characters: In summer dress the males with their bright red and black plumage are easily identified (see photograph on plate 16) although they may be confused with the Fire-crowned Bishop Bird. The latter, however, has a red forehead and black wings while the Red Bishop Bird has a black forehead and brownish or greyish wings. The females and males in winter plumage are more difficult to identify, but the birds are clearly streaked on the breast and lack the yellow or mustard coloured rump of the Yellow-rumped Widow Bird.

Distribution: Red Bishop Birds are very widely distributed in Zimbabwe wherever suitable habitat occurs. In summer they are associated with rank grass or reed beds, usually in moister areas. However, they may breed even on ant-hills or in cultivated lands where suitable grass grows. In the non-breeding season the birds may occur in almost any grassland.

Notes: During the non-breeding season the various *Euplectes* species tend to gather in large flocks perhaps even joining the queleas, and in this form move around over grassland in search of food. The exact extent of this movement is not yet clearly known, but it is certain that at least at the higher altitudes in Zimbabwe, the Red Bishop Bird disappears during the winter months. When breeding, the Red Bishop Bird may do so in loose colonies consisting of one or more males each with two or three females. Some colonies in reed beds may number thousands of birds. The oval nest of strips of grass or reed blade are built by the males and when the eggs are laid the nest is still so thinly walled that the eggs can be seen inside. The female lines the nest during the incubation period and by the time the chicks hatch the nest is very well lined with fine grass heads. The nests are generally rather poorly concealed and are therefore easily found. The males spend a great deal of time 'buzzing' over the nesting site with their feathers puffed up, or perching on prominent pieces of grass and fluffing up their feathers until they look like little balls (see photograph). Breeding takes place as soon as the grass and reeds have grown sufficiently high to support the nests, which usually means from about December onwards.

57 RED-COLLARED WIDOW BIRD (R.813)
Plate 14   *EUPLECTES ARDENS*

Field characters: The male in breeding plumage is readily identified by the black plumage with the red collar and the long soft tail. Note that the tail has ten elongated feathers whereas the whydahs have only four. The females and birds in winter dress have a very noticeable eyebrow and the breast is washed or suffused with yellow and is not streaked at all.

Distribution: The Red-collared Widow Bird is commonly found in damp grasslands over much of the eastern half of Zimbabwe.

Notes: Like the Red Bishop Bird, the male makes display flights over the nesting area, but does not fluff up its feathers to anything like the same extent. The display is carried out using the tail which is spread and pushed downwards as the bird flies along, with wings fully extended. By pushing the tail down the ends of the feathers are forced upwards by the air flow as the bird flies along. The Red-collared Widow Bird favours the moister grasslands and in fact very often you will find both the Red-collared and Red Bishop Birds nesting together. The Yellow-rumped Widow Bird, on the other hand, is generally found in drier areas. The Red-collared will join up with other widow birds in the non-breeding season and many thousands may gather at suitable roosts usually in reed beds over water. The nest is an oval one suspended in grass usually quite near the ground and is very much better hidden than that of the Red Bishop Bird.

58 ORANGE-BREASTED WAXBILL (R.838)
Plate 30   *AMANDAVA SUBFLAVA*

Field characters: This is a gregarious little bird which is seen in moist grassland or reed beds. If clearly seen the red bill and rump are very noticeable and the red eyebrow of the male is outstanding. The Orange-breasted Waxbills have a habit of shooting out of the grass, calling to one another with soft clear whistles, flying a short distance, and then dropping back into the grass. The orange colour is usually visible as they fly away.

Distribution: It is common and widespread in the east, but becomes less so westwards. Once again it is probably limited by the presence of suitable moist grasslands.

Notes: The birds usually occur in small flocks and they tend to keep in touch with one another with a soft twittering call which rises in volume when they are disturbed. Listen for the call as it serves as a guide to the birds which are otherwise not seen, as they forage in long grass. When disturbed the birds fly up out of the grass, fly a short distance, and then drop down into the grass again. If greatly disturbed they may fly up as a flock, buzz round a couple of times, and then disappear back into the grass some distance away. Unlike many other waxbills, they do not seem to spend a great deal of time feeding off the seed heads of grasses, but prefer to forage down on the ground or near the bases of plants. They nest in old widow or bishop bird nests, which they take over in the late summer and re-line with feathers and fine grass heads. It is not uncommon for both birds to be in the nest at the same time and, as the nests are built by a much larger bird, they readily accommodate both waxbills.

Grassland

The Zimbabwean grasslands are extremely variable in that the grass species may vary from area to area, but more particularly in that the length of grass varies according to the amount of rainfall available. We thus find that in the east the grass tends to be considerably longer and denser than the grasslands of the west. Nevertheless, you will find that the grasslands generally have similar species throughout, but you will also find that the species are very often determined by the length of grass. The Buffy Pipit, for example, favours relatively short open grasslands and seldom moves into areas with longer grass. The Rufous-naped Lark on the other hand is very much at home in the long grasses of the Mashonaland plateau and, in Mashonaland at least, is not normally found in areas of short grass.

The activities of farmers have resulted in the development of numerous new grasslands mainly in areas which were originally either woodland or tree savanna. This removal of the woodland and the development of grassland suitable for grazing must have resulted in the encouragement of the grassland species while woodland species have obviously decreased because of the destruction of their habitat.

The grassland areas at first glance often appear to offer relatively little in the way of bird life, particularly during the winter months. If you spend a little time searching around, however, you will find that within the grassland there are always areas which are more densely populated than others—probably associated with the availability of food. The various species of cisticola such as the Rattling Cisticola, described on page 72, are usually present throughout the year in any given area. The cisticolas are another group which is best identified by its calls and this therefore may result in some difficulty for people who are new at bird watching.

59 CATTLE EGRET (R.61)   *BUBULCUS IBIS*
Plate 17

Field characters: Cattle Egrets are relatively small egrets and are readily differentiated from the other white egrets in a variety of ways. First of all, the Cattle Egret is smaller and appears as a much more squat, heavily built bird. The neck is comparatively thicker and shorter than that of other egrets. Secondly, the Cattle Egret usually occurs in flocks or at least small parties while the other white egrets are generally more solitary birds, although they may gather in numbers at suitable feeding places. Thirdly, the Cattle Egret is a bird of the drier grasslands while the others are all birds of the vleis and waterways. The bill is yellow, but the legs vary in colour from a rather bright yellow during the breeding season to a rather dirty dark green in the rest of the year.

Distribution: The Cattle Egret may appear anywhere in Zimbabwe, but is subject to considerable movement.

Notes: It seems to be increasing in numbers in Zimbabwe and may well be extending its range as is happening in South Africa. To date, however, few breeding colonies have been discovered in Zimbabwe. Cattle Egrets are usually seen accompanying game or stock in open grassland, normally where the grass is not very long. They will walk through even very tall grass providing it is not too thick. The birds feed on insects such as grasshoppers disturbed by the animals as they feed across the veld and one may often see the birds running to catch insects thus disturbed. At night they gather in huge flocks at suitable roosts, normally in reed beds over water in dams or large rivers. They execute a remarkable series of manoeuvres as they come in to land spilling air rapidly in order to lose altitude. Nearly all the birds stop at the water's edge for a drink before moving into the reed beds to roost.

60 ABDIM'S STORK (R.78)   *CICONIA ABDIMII*
Plate 12

Field characters: The storks are distinguished from the egrets by their rather heavier bill and their heavier build. Abdim's Stork is, overall, a black bird with white belly and rump. The

Black Stork is similar but lacks the white rump and has a red bill which is very obvious even from a distance. Abdim's Stork normally occurs in flocks whereas the Black Stork is generally solitary or in pairs.

Distribution: Abdim's Stork, a summer visitor to the whole of Zimbabwe, breeds in the mountains of North and West Africa. It may be found in any area of open grassland during the summer.

Notes: This common migrant usually appears in late September or October in small to large flocks which may spend many hours circling on thermals. Many obviously go further south, but a lot spend their summer in the Zimbabwean veld looking for insects and small animals. They have become greatly attracted to cattle feeding lots where there are obviously many grubs and other forms of insect food and the photograph on plate 12 was taken at one of these. At these feeding lots they may become very tame and allow a very close approach.

61 BLACK KITE (R.128) *MILVUS M. MIGRANS*
YELLOW-BILLED KITE (R.129) *M.m.parasitus*
Plate 4

Field characters: These kites are usually seen drifting slowly along over the grasslands or along roads. Their general brown colour and the forked tail readily distinguish them. The Black Kite appears darker than the Yellow-billed Kite although the former's head is generally lighter. The yellow bill of the latter is very obvious if a good view is obtained. The tail is used to steer when gliding and is a useful field character.

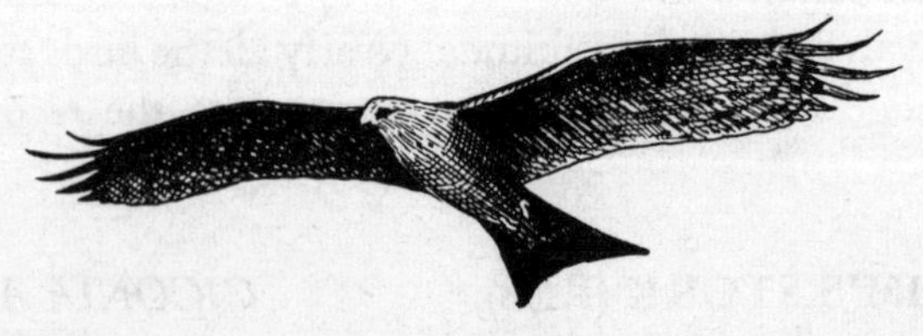

Distribution: The Black Kite is a migrant which may be seen during the rainy season, whereas the Yellow-billed Kite is resident, at least at lower altitudes, breeding during the early summer.

Notes: These two kites are placed as separate species by some authors and as sub-species by others. The Black Kite is not as common as the Yellow-billed Kite, but may perhaps be seen in more settled areas or even towns more often than the latter. The photograph on plate 4 shows both birds at a kill. They are often to be seen at the roadside eating animals killed by cars. While feeding they may become victims themselves. They are attracted to veld fires where they alight on the burnt ground to eat small animals and insects killed by the fire. When over grassland, they quarter the area at no great height, usually gliding gracefully along until prey is spotted when the bird drops into the grass quite slowly.

62 CROWNED PLOVER (R.242)
Plate 10   *VANELLUS CORONATUS*

Field characters: Like all the plovers, the Crowned Plover is a noisy bird which is readily identified by its distinctive call of 'Kiwiet', hence the Afrikaans name of Kiewietjie. When seen the white ring or crown on the head is usually very obvious.

Distribution: It is found throughout Zimbabwe in the areas having short open grassland and is probably resident, although some local movement certainly occurs.

Notes: The Crowned Plover occurs in pairs or small parties, but may occur in large flocks at certain times of the year. It has moved into the cultivated lands and has probably been extending its range in Zimbabwe as the woodlands are stumped out to make way for pastures or croplands. On bright moonlight nights it spends considerable time flying around screaming loudly and at this time it may appear in areas where it does not normally occur. It nests on the ground like all plovers, merely laying its eggs in a slight scrape in the ground. As can be seen from the photograph on plate 10 not only the eggs, but also the chicks are cryptically coloured and the chicks escape their enemies by lying absolutely still on the ground when they become almost invisible. The Kiewietjies will dive-bomb you if you approach the nest and will come close enough for you to feel the wind of their passage.

63 RUFOUS-NAPED LARK (R.458)
Plate 15   *MIRAFRA AFRICANA*

Field characters: The larks are, on the whole, rather difficult to identify, but the Rufous-naped Lark may be identified by its call which may be rendered 'Chiwicki-chiwi'. Particularly during the breeding season this call can be heard almost constantly where the Rufous-naped Lark occurs. The Rufous-naped Lark is a comparatively large lark with a fairly heavily streaked back and a distinct white eyebrow. The bill is quite heavy, certainly much heavier than that of the pipits.

Distribution: This bird is found over most of Zimbabwe wherever suitable savanna grassland occurs. It seems to prefer grassland with scattered trees, but the grass should not be too dense.

Notes: The male selects a perch from which it calls throughout the breeding season, and even during the non-breeding season it may call from this perch. The tops of ant-hills, bushes or fence posts are all utilised. It is a rather heavy flyer and is therefore readily distinguishable from many of the other common larks of Zimbabwe. The nest is a cup shaped one placed in grassland and normally has some form of dome as is shown in the photograph.

64 RATTLING CISTICOLA (R.642)
Plate 15   *CISTICOLA CHINIANA*

Field characters: The cisticolas, like the larks, are generally rather difficult to identify, but one must bear in mind the habitat, as this is one of the most important field characters. The call is important and the Rattling Cisticola spends a lot of time sitting on top of a bush or tree calling something which may be rendered as 'Chee-chee chichi-chirrrrr'. It also has a variety of other notes and calls, but these are usually interspersed with the call noted above. They are essentially dull brown birds with a dark brown back and lighter underparts. The top of the head is a russet colour and the sides of the head are a light brown (see photograph on plate 15).

Distribution: The Rattling Cisticola is found throughout Zimbabwe, merely being limited by the presence of suitable grasslands or open scrub.

Notes: This common cisticola will be found wherever grasslands occur, but is not normally found in the vleis where its place is taken by other species. It likes scattered trees or bushes from which it may call. It makes use of cultivated lands to a certain extent, but is probably more commonly met along the margins of the croplands unless these are lying fallow. They are very conspicuous birds because they always pop up to have a look at any intruder and attract attention to themselves by their loud alarm calls. The nest is a ball type, the outside of which is usually made up of very coarse grass blades lined with fine plant material.

65 BUFFY PIPIT (R.695)   *ANTHUS VAALENSIS*
Plate 13

Field characters: The pipits are another genus which is extremely difficult to identify in the field if one merely considers the colours of the various parts of the bird. Like the cisticolas the pipits occupy different habitats and have different habits. The Buffy Pipit may occur in the same areas as Richard's Pipit, but on the whole it prefers the more open grassland with tufts of grass fairly well spaced and is very often found in cultivated lands. It is a distinctly larger bird than Richard's Pipit and it has a much plainer, unstreaked back and chest. The outer tail feathers if seen are buff in colour whereas those of Richard's Pipit are white.

Distribution: This species is widely but locally distributed throughout Zimbabwe and as it exhibits local movement may turn up even in places where it does not normally occur.

Notes: The Buffy Pipit often wags its tail up and down, thus showing its relationship to the wagtails. When running on the ground it invariably wags its tail two or three times when it stops after each short run. When flushed the bird will not normally fly very far and again will wag its tail on alighting. It prefers to land on the ground, but will land in trees or bushes on occasion. The nest is a deep cup which is placed under a tuft of grass or under an overturned clod in ploughed land. I have found these birds nesting along the ridges in a tobacco land where both the plants and the soil provided some protection.

66 RED-BILLED QUELEA (R.805) *QUELEA QUELEA*
Plate 16

Field characters: During the breeding season the males have a black face and the rest of the head is washed with pink or red. As the birds breed only in the lowveld they are less likely to be seen in this condition than in the non-breeding condition which is illustrated in the plate. The red bill stands out and the light eyestripe can usually be seen. They normally occur in fairly small flocks on the plateau although very large numbers may gather at times, but in the lower lying areas of Zimbabwe huge flocks numbering many thousands and probably millions of birds may collect, particularly at roosts or where food is plentiful.

Distribution: The Red-billed Quelea occurs throughout Zimbabwe but is only a winter migrant to the plateau moving to the lowveld to breed during the summer.

Notes: Red-billed Queleas will come to bird tables to feed even in fairly well built-up areas and, because of the large numbers involved, they are real pests as they eat all the food before other birds have a chance. Weighing birds just before they go to roost and again the next morning, I have found that they may lose roughly two grams in weight out of a total body weight of 20 grams and it is noteworthy that in the evening the crop is greatly distended and filled with seeds. Where they nest they may gather in vast flocks, with nests covering practically every tree in the area. The nest is something like that of the Red Bishop Bird, but is much more roughly constructed and of much coarser material. When going to roost or coming down to drink the flocks chatter the whole time and where large numbers congregate, this noise can be heard from a considerable distance.

67 COMMON WAXBILL (R.843) *ESTRILDA ASTRILD*
Plate 28

Field characters: The generally barred appearance, red bill, and eyestripe readily distinguish this waxbill. The belly is also washed with red, the males being somewhat brighter than the females.

Distribution: This waxbill is common throughout Zimbabwe wherever suitable long grass occurs. It is normally associated with water, but not necessarily so.

Notes: The Common Waxbill is a gregarious bird which normally occurs in small parties, but which may occur in very large flocks at times. It has moved into gardens in both urban and rural areas and may become very tame where seed is put out for it. The birds in the party keep in touch with a quiet pinging whistle and when excited have a rather noisy call which might be rendered as 'Dee-dee dur dit'. The nest is a large rounded mass of grasses placed practically at ground level with a tunnel pointing downwards from the nest to the ground, usually hidden under a grass tuft or, in one case in my garden, under a pile of rubbish thrown out preparatory to making compost. On top of the nest a small porch is usually built which may be used at times by the birds. The Common Waxbill is parasitised by the Pin-tailed Whydah, but the waxbills do not suffer because the whydahs do not eject the young waxbills.

Tree savanna

Tree savanna represents a transitional type of habitat between the grasslands and the true woodlands. Here the trees or bushes are well scattered and thus do not form any type of canopy except possibly very locally. The trees which occur within these tree savannas are varied and in fact are normally representative of the woodlands of the area in which they occur. There seems to be some doubt as to whether these tree savannas are in fact natural or whether they are the result of man's removing the woodlands over large areas, thus allowing the grasslands to spread. Once again tree savanna type habitat is being developed by many farmers as they clear all but the largest trees in order to encourage grazing and increase the carrying capacity of their veld.

Many of the birds found in the tree savannas are those which feed either on the ground, within the grassland and then nest in the trees, such as the Secretary Bird, or those which use the trees as perches from which they can either hawk insects, for example, the bee-eaters, or pounce on insects on the ground below, such as the Lilac-breasted Roller. Obviously one must also expect to find within these regions any birds which normally occur within the grasslands proper or within the woodlands proper. Birds after all have wings and are therefore very mobile and can move from their chosen habitats for brief periods into the adjoining habitats.

The tree savannas in Zimbabwe probably fall into three basic types: those with fairly long grass and scattered large trees mostly of the miombo woodland type; those with short open grass with either acacia or miombo species; and those with very short rather sparse grass with essentially acacia species being the tree variety. In each case one can expect the birds of the different types of woodland to be those most likely to occur apart from those listed on the following pages.

Plate 17

117 Black Eagle
34″/850 mm   *Peter Steyn*

77   Martial Eagle
32″/800 mm   *Alan Kemp*

Plate 18

35   Fish Eagle
28″/700 mm   *Bill Nichol*

71   Bateleur
24″/600 mm   *Eliot Lyons*

72　Namaqua Dove ♂ and ♀
9½″/240 mm　　*Geoff McIlleron*

80　Turtle Dove
11″/275 mm　　*Geoff McIlleron*

Plate 19

81　Meyer's Parrot
9″/225 mm　　*Peter Ginn*

82　Fiery-necked Nightjar
9½″/237 mm　　*Bill Nichol*

84 Crested Barbet
9″/225 mm   *Peter Ginn*

85 Golden-tailed Woodpecker
8″/200 mm   *Bill Nichol*

Plate 20

87 Fork-tailed Drongo
10″/250 mm   *Bill Nichol*

89 Black-headed Oriole
10″/250 mm   *Cyril Laubscher*

86 Lesser Striped Swallow
    6½"/165 mm   *Alan Kemp*

Plate 21

90 Grey-cheeked Tit
    6"/150 mm   *Peter Ginn*

93 Long-billed Crombec
    4"/100 mm   *Bill Nichol*

95 White-flanked Batis ♀
    5"/125 mm   *Cyril Laubscher*

88   African Golden Oriole ♂ 9″/225 mm   *Peter Ginn*

Plate 22

88   African Golden Oriole ♀ 9″/225 m

92   Groundscraper Thrush 8½″/212 mm   *Peter Ginn*

94 Black Flycatcher
8″/200 mm   *Peter Ginn*

96 Black-crowned Tchagra
9″/225 mm   *Bill Nichol*

Plate 23

97 White Helmet Shrike
8″/200 mm   *Bill Nichol*

98 Plum-coloured Starling ♂
7″/175 mm   *Peter Ginn*

78 Lizard Buzzard 14″/350 mm   *Bill Nichol*

Plate 24

113 Augur Buzzard 19″/475 mm   *Peter Steyn*

115 Malachite Sunbird ♂ 9″/225 mm   *Cyril Laubscher*

68 WHITE STORK (R.80)　　　　　　*CICONIA CICONIA*
Plate 12

Field characters: This is the only wholly white stork with black flight feathers which gives it the appearance of a black lower back and sides when standing (see plate 12). The red bill is also usually very obvious.

Distribution: The White Stork is a migrant which is found from October to March throughout the country.

Notes: The White Stork usually occurs in flocks or small parties, but even single birds often occur, perhaps in association with Abdim's Stork. They are to be found in open grassland with scattered trees or sometimes in marshy areas. Like Abdim's Stork they are often seen circling on the thermals, particularly in October and November and again in late February or March. They migrate to Europe to breed, although some breeding has taken place in South Africa. Some birds winter in Zimbabwe, but so far there has been no evidence of their breeding here. They feed mainly on insects, particularly locusts, and are therefore of great value to man.

69 SECRETARY BIRD (R.105)
Plate 12　　　　　　*SAGITTARIUS SERPENTARIUS*

Field characters: The plate shows a juvenile bird on the nest and shows quite clearly some of the main field characters of this species. On the back of the head the feathers which form a crest, and can be raised or lowered, are one of the most important field characters. The down-curved bill and the long legs with the black feathers on the thighs are also distinctive. The two elongated central tail feathers may or may not be visible, but in flight they give the bird a characteristic outline which immediately distinguishes it. The Secretary Bird is, overall, a grey bird with distinct black lower back caused by the black primaries.

Distribution: Although this bird occurs throughout Zimbabwe, with the exception of the Zambezi Valley, it is somewhat localised and may be absent from large areas of seemingly suitable country. It prefers open grassland with scattered trees, but may move into light woodland at times.

Notes: The Secretary Bird is probably best known for its habit of catching and eating snakes, but in fact snakes probably form a relatively small part of its diet. Insects, small mammals, and perhaps birds probably represent a far greater proportion of its diet. Secretary Birds are usually seen stalking across the veld in search of prey and one of their most characteristic features is the way in which they run with their wings outspread, prior to taking off. They normally occur in pairs and if you see one you should find another one nearby. The nest is usually built into the top of a thorn tree. The whole top of the tree is stamped down to leave a sort of halo around the nest which serves to hide the nest very effectively. This halo is clearly seen in the photograph on plate 12. When sitting, the bird crouches low in the nest so that you cannot see it and it will not leave the nest unless you actually climb up to it. Fortunately Secretary Birds are still quite common. Most farmers tend to protect them as they do so much good on the farm.

70 BLACK-SHOULDERED KITE (R.130)
ELANUS CAERULEUS

Field characters: This small hawk is the only one which is plain grey in colour except for the very noticeable black shoulders. If the bird is clearly seen the red eye is also very noticeable. Its hunting technique is also characteristic (see line drawing).

Distribution: It is found throughout Zimbabwe and is generally common in the more open grasslands with scattered trees. Certainly in Mashonaland it is the most common bird of prey in this habitat.

Notes: The Black-shouldered Kite is usually seen flying fairly slowly across the country, stopping to hover whenever it sees anything on the ground below. The bird usually hovers before dropping down onto the prey below and it may stop several times on the way down before actually dropping the last 3 or 4 metres into the grass. It will feed on small rodents, lizards, insects and so on, with mice being the dominant prey. The Black-shouldered Kite is generally protected by farmers as it is not known to take poultry and probably seldom if ever catches any birds. The Black-shouldered Kite is often collected by beginners in falconry as it becomes tame relatively quickly, but if reared from a chick it is a rather noisy bird. The nest is usually placed fairly high up in a tree in the middle of an open area. It is not a very substantial nest, usually made of bits of stick and lined with finer material.

71 BATELEUR (R.151) *TERATHOPIUS ECAUDATUS*
Plate 18

Field characters: The Bateleur is usually seen gliding over open country, and in the air the short tail and long pointed wings are very obvious and form the best field characters for this species. Even when the bird is sitting the short tail is very obvious (see photograph on plate 18) and the colours are probably better seen under these circumstances. In flight the black and white pattern, the body and trailing edges of the wings being black or rather dark and the rest of the wings being white, is also a useful guide to the adult males, although the young are duller.

Distribution: The Bateleur may occur anywhere in Zimbabwe, but tends to prefer the open parkland to well wooded or forested areas.

Notes: This eagle is essentially a scavenger and therefore cannot find food easily in areas with a full canopy of trees. It is also probably the most accomplished of the soaring birds and it is very unusual to see a Bateleur flapping its wings except in the early morning and late evening when there are no thermals. It is certainly more adept at using these thermals than vultures. It seldom spends much time circling on thermals and is usually to be seen traversing the country at a fairly fast rate searching the ground below for carrion. It also kills a certain number of smaller mammals and snakes. It is one of the distinctive features of Wankie where there is at least one in sight at most times.

72 NAMAQUA DOVE (R.318)　　　　*OENA CAPENSIS*
Plate 19

Field characters: The only dove with a rather long tail, it has the typically fast flight of the species. The male is distinguished by the black bib and face (see plate 19) while the female has a rather white face.

Distribution: The Namaqua Dove is found over most of Zimbabwe although it has only rarely been recorded on the higher parts of the plateau and may well be entirely absent from the Eastern Districts. It becomes more common westwards, and in drier areas is one of the most common birds.

Notes: Namaqua Doves must drink every day and may gather in large numbers at favourite pools or drinking places at about mid-morning. There is a continual stream of birds coming and going to and from the water hole. When feeding they walk around with the tail held off the ground and they have the very typical, rather bobbing, rolling walk of all doves. The call is a rather low 'Hooo' which has remarkable carrying power. The nest is usually placed very low down in a bush or small tree and may be made either of small twigs or even grass occasionally and is usually rather more solid than that of other doves. The eggs are a creamy colour and are quite small.

Field characters: This wholly grey lourie is probably most easily identified by its characteristic call of 'Go-way', the 'way' being drawn out at times. The long tail and rather thin crest make identification, even in silhouette, relatively simple.

Distribution: The Go-way-bird is probably more common in thornveld savanna than in other areas, but it is very widespread in Zimbabwe and can in fact even turn up in well developed brachystegia woodland.

Notes: The Grey Lourie is probably the best known of the louries as it is so widespread and it certainly makes its presence heard wherever it occurs. It has a rather slow laborious flight and at times it almost looks as though it is losing the battle to stay airborne. Grey Louries occur in small groups or parties which move around looking for fruit, insects, and so on, near the tops of trees. Like all louries they are very agile in the tree tops, running along the branches and jumping from branch to branch. The nest is a platform of fairly thin sticks, many of them very thorny, looking rather like a well developed dove's nest. Two or three eggs are laid and these can be seen from below.

74 CARMINE BEE-EATER (R.407)
Plate 11   *MEROPS NUBICOIDES*

Field characters: Like all the bee-eaters the Carmine Bee-eater has a well developed somewhat curved bill and generally catches insects on the wing from a prominent perch. The Carmine Bee-eater is one of the species which has the central tail feathers greatly elongated. The general carmine colour and green head make this species relatively easy to identify in the field. The call which is a double noted 'Derk-derk' is also distinctive.

Distribution: This intertropical migrant appears in about August and immediately starts clearing out the nest holes for breeding. It is found throughout Zimbabwe, but is not normally common in the higher areas and is only sporadically seen in the Eastern Districts.

Notes: These beautiful birds nest in huge colonies, the most famous of which is the one near Beatrice, but larger colonies occur in various parts of the lowveld of Zimbabwe. At the colony the birds are remarkably tame and will sit on a perch near the nests within 4 to 5 metres of an observer. They move throughout the surrounding countryside in search of prey during the day and they gather again to roost near the colony at night. After breeding, the birds disperse over most of Zimbabwe and may in fact turn up almost anywhere at this time. Like the rollers they are often attracted to veld fires where they hawk the insects chased up by the fire. Bee-eaters have remarkable eyesight and I have known a Carmine Bee-eater to fly over my head while it was hawking insects I could not see. Having started from a perch over 100 metres away, the bird could obviously see the insect while I could not see it from a distance of about 10 to 15 metres.

75 LILAC-BREASTED ROLLER (R.413)
Plate 11   *CORACIAS CAUDATA*

Field characters: The strong bill and long thin pin feathers on the outside of the tail are important field characters. When clearly seen the lilac breast and blue wings immediately distinguish this bird from other similar ones. In flight this is one of our most beautiful birds with blue wings and tail and orange coloured back.

Distribution: The Lilac-breasted Roller is very widespread in Zimbabwe and is generally quite common where it occurs. It is probably most common in the thornveld savannas, but it will occur anywhere where there is suitable open grassland with scattered trees and bushes. It does not normally move into well-developed woodland where its place is taken by the other rollers.

Notes: The Lilac-breasted Roller is a rather noisy bird at times and thus often draws attention to itself by its rather harsh calls. It can do the most remarkable aerial acrobatics although these are probably performed mainly during the breeding season. It sits on a conspicuous perch from which it surveys the surrounding countryside and when it spots an insect on the ground it drops down onto it with a characteristic wing action, the wings being held high above the back. It usually eats the insect immediately although it may carry it back to its perch. Lilac-breasted Rollers normally occur in pairs, but small family parties may occur in an area. Large numbers gather at bush fires where they prove adept at catching insects in the air. They nest in a hole in a tree, usually fairly high up, and little attempt is made to disguise the presence of the nest.

76 MASKED WEAVER (R.803) *PLOCEUS VELATUS*
Plate 16

Field characters: In the summer the males with their bright yellow plumage, red eyes and black faces are readily distinguishable from all but the other two similar species. They differ from the Spotted-backed and Lesser Masked Weavers by the yellow of the crown reaching forward in front of the eye and the back being comparatively plain. The females and non-breeding birds are rather nondescript and are easily confused with the other weavers.

Distribution: This bird is widely distributed throughout Zimbabwe with the possible exception of the higher areas in the east.

Notes: The Masked Weaver will turn up almost anywhere, but it is definitely a bird which favours the parkland savanna particularly those areas where acacia trees are present. The birds are nearly always associated with water during the breeding season and if possible they like to build their nests over water. They have adapted to man's gardens and are often found nesting over fish ponds or swimming baths. The Masked Weaver does not seem to nest in the huge colonies which one finds in South Africa, but more often in scattered groups of one or two males and half a dozen females, with four or five nests being occupied at any one time. Larger colonies do occur in certain areas particularly in the lower lying parts of Zimbabwe. The male constructs the basic shell of the nest before the female takes over and lines the nest very warmly with fine grass heads. It is interesting to note that the eggs of the Masked Weaver are tremendously variable being plain white, white with pink or mauve spots, through green to blue, also with or without spots and blotches.

Miombo woodland

The term miombo is one which is not widely used by laymen in Zimbabwe, but it is synonymous with the term brachystegia woodland. The term miombo is one which is applied to the woodlands of tropical Africa which are dominated by the various brachystegia species particularly *Brachystegia spiciformis* above approximately 1 000 metres above sea level, by *Brachystegia boehmi* below 1 000 metres and by *Baikiaea plurijuga* in the west. Thus this term encompasses all the brachystegia woodlands of Zimbabwe. The species of trees associated with the brachystegia species are members of the genera *Julbernardia*, *Isoberlinia* and *Berlinia*. Typical trees would include the msasa, mnondo, and so on.

The miombo woodlands vary from areas of mature woodland where you find large trees which form a fairly continuous canopy over short and sparse grasses, through more open woodland with smaller trees, to scrub and bush which have comparatively little grass and in which the grass is of minor importance. In Mashonaland I have found that the areas of mature brachystegia are those which tend to have the greatest variety and concentration of birds and I have always presumed that this is because of the presence of abundant food. Around Marondera, I have also noticed that those woodlands dominated by the msasa tree are usually the most interesting while the mnondo is not particularly favoured by many birds. Areas of almost pure mahobahoba are rather uninteresting and you will find that there is only a limited number of species in these areas except perhaps during the fruiting season when a variety of species gather to eat the fruit.

The miombo woodlands contain a large variety of birds most of which are insectivorous as there seem to be few seeds which are suitable for birds to eat. One of the most interesting features of the smaller birds in this habitat is their habit of joining up into parties during the non-breeding season and moving through the woodland in this form with each species searching for insects in a different niche within the habitat. The woodpeckers work their way along the larger branches and trunks while the crombecs and batises work through the leaves. There may well be a certain amount of symbiotic relationship here with the different species helping one another, in that insects disturbed by one species may well be caught by another species working under slightly different circumstances. These bird parties are quite important to the bird watcher because in the non-breeding season you can walk through a large area of woodland without seeing any bird species unless you find a bird party. The best way to locate the bird parties is to listen for them, particularly the calls of the Grey-cheeked Tits and possibly the Black-headed Orioles as well. Once you have found a bird party it can be followed over quite considerable distances and the different species may be observed in fairly leisurely fashion provided you do not come so close to the birds as to disturb them. When disturbed, bird parties tend to break up and may take some time to reform.

During the summer months the miombo woodlands are noisy places as quite a number of the species which occur here are noisy birds and in this way draw attention to themselves. The Black-headed Oriole can be heard whistling almost anywhere where suitable woodland occurs. At night the Fiery-necked Nightjar can be heard calling with its very distinctive 'Good Lord deliver us'. I feel that this habitat is one where the use of bird calls is probably very much more important than most others, the forests being the only one where calls are even more important. There are a number of records available which contain many of the species listed below and if you have a record player it may well be worth your while to invest in these records in order to be able to learn the calls before you go into the field.

77 MARTIAL EAGLE (R.142)
Plate 18   *POLEMAETUS BELLICOSUS*

Field characters: This magnificent eagle is usually identified by the dark bib and upper breast, and the spotted lower breast and belly. It may be confused with the smaller Black-breasted Snake Eagle, but it may be distinguished in flight by the dark wings and tail of the Martial Eagle contrasting with the barred wings and tail of the Snake Eagle.

Distribution: The Martial Eagle is found throughout Zimbabwe and perhaps surprisingly is still fairly common in most areas.

Notes: The Martial Eagle is one of our larger eagles and has been accused of most of the crimes for which eagles are said to be responsible. It lives mainly on the larger ground birds and mammals such as dassies and hares, but is probably not averse to eating carrion if this is available. It is probably not responsible for the killing of lambs or other domestic stock. The Martial Eagle favours the more open woodland areas and certainly moves out over the parkland savanna. Each pair needs a very large area for its hunting activities and therefore these eagles are never likely to become common. They build a large nest of sticks near the top of a tree and successful nests are used year after year.

78 LIZARD BUZZARD (R.144)
Plate 24   *KAUPIFALCO MONOGRAMMICUS*

Field characters: There are a number of small raptors which have the general grey colour of the Lizard Buzzard, but none of them has the black streak on the white chin which is clearly visible in the photograph on plate 24. The white bar on the tail is also a useful field character if the bird is seen from behind.

Distribution: This is quite a common bird in the woodlands of Zimbabwe and may occur almost anywhere in suitable woodland.

Notes: The Lizard Buzzard has a distinctive call consisting of a series of whistling notes uttered on a descending scale. It usually sits near the middle of a tree and when disturbed drops down to fly fairly close to the ground before swooping up to land in another tree. When flying it often glides between bouts of flapping. It probably feeds mainly on rats, lizards, and snakes, but insects must also form an important part of its diet at times. The stick nest is often placed very high in a tree and is usually lined with fine grasses or green leaves. It is interesting that the Lizard Buzzard is one of the few birds of prey which does not frighten small birds and it is very seldom mobbed by birds such as bulbuls or drongos.

79 CROWNED GUINEA-FOWL (R.192)
Plate 17   *NUMIDA MELEAGRIS*

Field characters: The Crowned Guinea-fowl is very well known to anybody who has spent even a short while in the bush as it is found in woodland and in most areas where there is grassland with trees. The shape, with the rather heavy body and the tail curving down towards the ground, is probably the best field character. If clearly seen the general blue plumage with white spots and the casque on top of the head are also distinctive.

Distribution: This bird is found throughout Zimbabwe except in unsuitable habitat and in the higher areas of the east.

Notes: Crowned Guinea-fowl normally move around in small to large flocks except during the breeding season when the birds pair off. The flocks can usually be found in the same general area all the year round and it appears that each flock has a fairly well defined circuit which it follows each day while feeding. The birds in the flock seem to spend a lot of time chasing one another and this is particularly noticeable when they are feeding on ploughed lands. In farming areas they seem to like to feed in the lands just prior to going to roost, and in the weeks immediately following planting they may consume considerable numbers of mealie pips. Breeding starts as soon as the grass has grown sufficiently to provide suitable cover for the nests and the flocks then split up into pairs with each pair selecting a certain area in which to breed. The nest is a deep hollow in fairly dense grass or near thick bush, usually in such a position that the bird can slip away unseen at the approach of danger. The eggs are very shiny and thick shelled with very obvious pits in the surface. They are rather noisy birds and their call may be heard at almost any time of the day and night, but they are particularly noisy in the early morning and occasionally in the evening. If a flock is scattered they call to one another with a rather high, thin, piping whistle and in this way the flock gathers again. By imitating this whistle, the guinea-fowl can be called in to an observer.

80 CAPE TURTLE DOVE (R.316)
Plate 19   *STREPTOPELIA CAPICOLA*

Field characters: The typical dove shape and bill are obvious in
this species and in general the bird is the most uniformly coloured
of the doves with a ring on the back of the neck. The lower third
of the tail is white and it lacks the red eye of the Red-eyed Dove
with which it may be confused. The call is also characteristic.

Distribution: The Cape Turtle Dove is found throughout Zimbabwe, but probably does not become as plentiful as the
Laughing Dove locally. In areas where woodlands or plant-
ations have developed fully its place may be taken by the
Red-eyed Dove.

Notes: This dove is extremely well known, but it does not seem
to have adapted to man's gardens in the way that the Laughing
Dove has. It generally favours more open woodland where it
can find clear ground for feeding. When walking on the ground
it has a peculiar bobbing action of the head which is also useful
in the identification of this species. At Peterhouse we have found
that as the trees planted in all the gardens have matured so the
Cape Turtle Dove has decreased in numbers and the Red-eyed
Dove has become dominant. The Turtle Dove has a display
flight similar to that of the Red-eyed Dove during which the
bird towers into the air with clapping wings and then sets the
wings for planing downward to the trees below.

81 MEYER'S PARROT (R.327) *POICEPHALUS MEYERI*
Plate 19

Field characters: Meyer's Parrot has the broad, hooked bill so
characteristic of all parrots, but in the field the feature which I
think is the best for identification is the rather heavy blunt head
and very rapid wing beat in flight. The wings have a pointed
appearance and Meyer's Parrot has a fairly strident whistle
'Chee-chee-chee' which is audible at considerable distances. The
belly and rump are a greenish blue varying quite considerably
from ultramarine through to an almost pure green. The head and
wings have yellow patches which are also characteristic if seen.

Distribution: Except in the extreme south-east where it is replaced by the Brown-headed Parrot, Meyer's Parrot is found in all well developed woodland throughout Zimbabwe.

Notes: Meyer's Parrot favours well developed woodland where it can find suitable branches in which to build the nest hole. It would appear that it lays the eggs some three to four days apart as all the chicks in the nest are at different stages of development. It feeds on fruits, berries, and other seeds and I have noticed that it eats many of the seedpods of trees, such as the acacia, while they are green. The pod is held in one of the feet and is then torn up with the bill. When climbing or clambering around in a tree, it uses its beak as an extra 'hand' and this again is a feature which is characteristic of all parrots.

82 FIERY-NECKED NIGHTJAR (R.373)
Plate 19   *CAPRIMULGUS PECTORALIS*

Field characters: It is well nigh impossible to identify, with certainty, this species in the field unless the call is heard. The call is a clear quavering 'Good Lord deliver us'. In the hand the Fiery-necked Nightjar is readily identifiable because the wing emargination occurs within the white spots of the wing bar. This species does have rather more white on the wing and the lower part of the tail than other species, but this is a very variable characteristic.

Distribution: The Fiery-necked Nightjar is widely distributed in woodlands throughout Zimbabwe.

Notes: The eggs are usually laid in a cleared area amongst leaves under trees. They are a clear shell pink although they may have a few spots of a slightly darker pink scattered over them. They do not normally have any clouding or marking of darker pink, grey or mauve. In this respect they are quite different from the eggs of other similar species. When sitting on the ground the Nightjar relies on its cryptic colouring for protection—it will sit very tight and merely let you walk past unless you get very close. If it does fly up it 'flutters' away quite silently to alight again at at no great distance. In flight the white wing spots and tail are usually very obvious.

Field characters: The hornbills, as their name suggests, have rather large horny bills, but Grey Hornbills do not have a particularly noticeable casque on the top of their bills, although it is present in the male. They are the only hornbills with very drab grey and off-white plumage and this makes their identification relatively simple.

Distribution: They are the only hornbills found in the brachystegia of the plateau, but will also occur in the wooded areas of the lower lying parts of Zimbabwe in association with other hornbills such as the Yellow-billed Hornbill.

Notes: The slow dipping flight and clear whistling call usually attract attention to this species. It would appear to be fairly localised in its distribution although such movement probably occurs at certain times of the year. Once again it seems to prefer the well developed woodlands rather than scrub although in the west I have seen these birds in scrublands as well. Hornbills have the peculiar habit of sealing the female inside the nest and during her internment she undergoes a complete moult. Despite the size

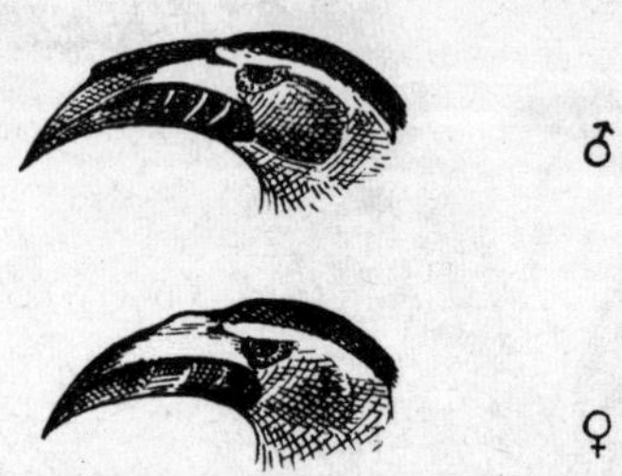

of the bird it is able to squeeze through an incredibly small hole and the nest entrance is seldom more than 40 mm to 50 mm wide by 80 mm long. Grey Hornbills seem to prefer to move around in pairs, at least this is certainly true in Mashonaland, whereas other species occur in large noisy flocks. In the west, however, the Grey Hornbill can form quite large flocks on occasions.

84 CRESTED BARBET (R.439)
Plate 20   *TRACHYPHONUS VAILLANTII*

Field characters: The crest and heavy build and bill distinguish this species. The plumage appears to be rather mottled in a variety of different colours (see plate 20). The long drawn out purring trill which sounds something like an alarm clock is also characteristic and often draws attention to the bird.

Distribution: The Crested Barbet would appear to be present in practically any woodland with reasonably sized trees, below about 1 700 metres. They are often fairly localised in their distribution, however.

Notes: Crested Barbets are normally found in pairs throughout the year and each pair can usually be found in the same area at

100 Pied Barbet
7″/175 mm   *Peter Ginn*

102 Long-tailed Shrike
19″/475 mm   *Cyril Laubscher*

Plate 25

104 Red-shouldered Starling
10″/250 mm   *Peter Ginn*

21 Blue-eared Starling
9″/225 mm   *Peter Ginn*

101 Crimson-breasted Shrike 9"/225 mm *Cyril Laubscher*

Plate 26

103 White-crowned Shrike 9"/225 mm *Peter Ginn*

121 Boulder Chat 10"/250 mm *Bill Nichol*

106   Double-banded Sandgrouse ♂   10″/250 mm   *G. Arnott*

Plate 27

2   Laughing Dove   10″/250 mm   *Bill Nichol*

107   Red-billed Hornbill   18″/450 mm   *Alan Kemp*

111 Cape Batis ♂
4½″/112 mm   *Bill Nichol*

111 Cape Batis ♀
4½″/112 mm   *Peter Ginn*

Plate 28

14 Blue Waxbill
5″/125 mm   *Peter Ginn*

67 Common Waxbill
5″/125 mm   *Geoff McIlleron*

6   Black-eyed Bulbul
8″/200 mm   *Bill Nichol*

91   Arrow-marked Babbler
9″/225 mm   *Peter Ginn*

Plate 29

109 Olive Thrush
8½″/215 mm   *Geoff McIlleron*

110 Cape Robin
7″/175 mm   *Peter Ginn*

17   Wire-tailed Swallow   5″/125 mm   *W. T. Miller*

Plate 30

58   Orange-breasted Waxbill ♂ and ♀ 4″/100 mm   *Laubscher*

112   East African Swee   3½″/90 mm   *Cyril Laubscher*

43 Swainson's Francolin
15″/375 mm   *Cyril Laubscher*

51 African Marsh Harrier
18″/450 mm   *Peter Ginn*

Plate 31

108 Yellow-billed Hornbill
22″/550 mm   *Alan Kemp*

119 Spotted Eagle Owl
18″/450 mm   *Bill Nichol*

116 Rock Kestrel
13″/325 mm   *Bill Nichol*

118 Rock Pigeon
13″/325 mm   *Peter Ginn*

Plate 32

120 Rock Nightjar
11″/275 mm   *Peter Ginn*

22   Red-winged Starling ♀
10″/250 mm   *Peter Ginn*

all times. The birds seem to spend a considerable amount of time calling and this is very often the first inkling one has of the presence of this species. They will feed quite readily on mealie meal at a bird table, but seem to prefer the mealie meal to be dunked in milk. It is very amusing to watch the Crested Barbet feeding as it often selects pieces of mealie meal which are much too large for it to swallow, but it still insists on trying to do so. The contortions and problems this causes are quite amazing. This barbet nests in a hole drilled in a tree and the same nest may be used year after year.

85 GOLDEN-TAILED WOODPECKER (R.447)
Plate 20   *CAMPETHERA ABINGONI*

Field characters: When trying to identify a woodpecker it is most important to note two things. First of all the relative size should be noted and secondly you should note whether the breast is barred, streaked or spotted. If these two features are noted then you should be able to identify any woodpecker in Zimbabwe. The Golden-tailed Woodpecker is a medium sized bird with a streaked breast, the black streaks running from top to tail. The amount of red on the head may be used to confirm the identification, but it may lead to confusion in making the initial diagnosis. Woodpeckers also have a characteristic flight pattern in which they beat their wings rapidly half a dozen times and then glide with the wings closed.

Distribution: The Golden-tailed Woodpecker is quite common in the miombo woodlands of the east, and in the west it makes use of both miombo woodlands and acacia wherever these are well developed. This means that it is usually found associated with riverine growth in the extreme west.

Notes: The Golden-tailed Woodpecker is typical of all woodpeckers in that it has the infuriating habit of keeping the tree between itself and you. The best way to overcome this is to stand still and either wait until the woodpecker reappears or get somebody to walk round the tree at a distance thus causing the woodpecker to move round to you. Woodpeckers' toes are set in a peculiar way: the inner and outer ones are directed backwards and the two middle ones directed forwards. This enables them to grip the surface of trees very strongly and they stabilise themselves with their tail. In this way they are able to hammer at the tree bark with their beak in order to get at the insects inside. The tapping of the bill often warns you that there is a woodpecker in the area as this noise carries considerable distances. The call is a rather harsh penetrating 'Waaa' which is often uttered as the bird flies away.

86 LESSER-STRIPED SWALLOW (R.503)
Plate 21   *HIRUNDO ABYSSINICA*

Field characters: The dark breast is very obvious whether the bird is at rest or flying overhead and this is probably the most useful field character. The streaking is very dark and the streaks themselves are comparatively thick. If a clear view is obtained the rufous ear coverts (see plate 21) are also obvious. The swallows of course may be distinguished from the swifts by their slower flight and more rounded wings (see page 30).

Distribution: The Lesser-striped Swallow may occur anywhere in Zimbabwe where there are suitable woodlands with rocks, culverts, or buildings under which it can build its nest.

Notes: The nest is made of mud pellets, the mud being mixed with saliva to give it strength, in the form of a bowl with a long tunnel. The eggs are laid in the bowl which is well lined with fine rootlets and if feathers can be seen in the nest it means that the nest has been taken over by swifts. The Lesser-striped Swallow has a rather slow undulating flight and it seems to spend a considerable amount of time gliding. The call which is uttered both in flight and at rest is a fairly light 'Tee-tee-tee' and this is a useful field character and often draws attention to the bird.

87 FORK-TAILED DRONGO (R.517)
Plate 20   *DICRURUS ADSIMILIS*

Field characters: This is the largest of the three similar wholly black woodland species in Zimbabwe. They are distinguishable from the other two by the deeply forked tail and the red eye. The most important field character, however, is their habit of hawking insects from a prominent perch. They are also much more noisy than the Black Cuckoo Shrike or Black Flycatcher.

Distribution: This bird may occur anywhere in Zimbabwe where there are suitable woodlands and although it may move into grassland areas particularly when fires occur, it is seldom found any distance from trees.

Notes: The Fork-tailed Drongo is a noisy, aggressive bird which soon draws attention to itself. It will not hesitate to mob birds of prey or snakes. It is sometimes to be seen riding on the backs of domestic animals or buck, hawking insects disturbed by the animals' feet. Beekeepers do not like drongos because they can, and I have seen them do this, pick off the bees emerging from a hive. The bee is caught in the air usually about 3 or 4 metres from the hive.

88 AFRICAN GOLDEN ORIOLE (R.520)
Plate 22   *ORIOLUS AURATUS*

Field characters: The bright yellow plumage of the male, with the black eye stripe which extends through the eye, is quite distinctive. Note that the wing primaries have some yellow on the outer web whereas the European Golden Oriole is only black. The female is a rather drab greenish yellow and is therefore often overlooked.

Distribution: Although some of the birds do remain throughout the winter, this species is essentially a summer visitor. It prefers well developed miombo woodland, particularly where large msasa trees are abundant. It may be very common locally.

Notes: The males are very noisy during the summer months and can usually be traced by their calls. The call is similar to that of the Black-headed Oriole, but is sufficiently different to be distinctive. The nest is made of grass and lichen and other material slung in a form of a hammock in the outer forks of a tree such as a msasa. The chicks are fed numerous caterpillars and on one occasion I watched a male trying to feed its chicks a caterpillar which was nearly 50 mm in length. He battered the caterpillar to a pulp and managed to get about a third of it into the chick's mouth. The chick lay with the other two-thirds hanging out of its beak for about ten minutes when it gave a convulsive swallow and another third disappeared down its throat. About quarter of an hour later the final third was also swallowed.

89 BLACK-HEADED ORIOLE (R.521)
Plate 20   *ORIOLUS LARVATUS*

Field characters: If it is clearly seen, the yellow plumage with the black head and pink bill make identification of this species easy in the field. The call is characteristic and is a loud whistle 'Phee-eoooo'.

Distribution: Although not present in the higher parts of the Eastern Districts it can be found almost anywhere else in Zimbabwe where well developed woodland occurs.

Notes: The Black-headed Oriole is resident and may be heard calling at any time of the year, although it is probably noisier in summer than at other times. The nest is a hammock like that of the Golden Oriole, but is normally made almost entirely of 'Old man's beard', and is usually higher than that of the Golden Oriole. Black-headed Orioles sometimes join bird parties in winter and then usually search the upper branches of trees.

90 GREY-CHEEKED TIT (R.526)
Plate 21   *PARUS GRISEIVENTRIS*

Field characters: The Grey-cheeked Tit is easy to identify if it is clearly seen because of the general grey colour and black crown and throat. The habit of creeping around on the branches and even up the trunk searching for insects is also a good guide to this species.

Distribution: This bird is confined to the brachystegia woodlands of northern Mashonaland where it may be quite common.

Notes: The Grey-cheeked Tit has taken over as nest sites many of the poles which man erects, fence poles, tennis court poles, and so on are very commonly used. In areas where these artificial nest sites do not occur it builds a nest in a hole in a tree. The bird usually has a favourite perch somewhere near the nesting site where it stops to check for danger before actually approaching the nest. Grey-cheeked Tits normally occur in pairs although small groups may be encountered and they usually join bird parties in the winter months. I have found that the calling of the tits very often leads one to a bird party which might otherwise have been missed.

91 ARROW-MARKED BABBLER (R.533)
Plate 29   *TURDOIDES JARDINEII*

Field characters: As this is the only babbler which is commonly found over most of Zimbabwe the calls should immediately serve to identify it. In the west where the Pied Babbler occurs there should be no confusion, as the Arrow-marked Babbler is an essentially brownish bird with very obvious white arrows on the breast.

Distribution: Although found throughout Zimbabwe, this species is generally confined to well wooded areas, but has become quite common in rural gardens in many parts of the country.

Notes: The babblers normally move round in parties of three to ten or twelve birds and seem to spend a lot of time searching for food either on the ground or in low bushes. When moving from one tree or bush to another, they generally start from the top of the bush and, gliding as much as possible, fly down near the base of the next bush or tree. The birds of the flock keep in touch with a low chirring call, but periodically the whole flock joins together to make their babbling sound which can be extremely loud when large numbers of birds are all doing it together. The groups are strongly territorial and a group will rapidly come to investigate a playback of a recording of a flock calling. The birds seem to have only one or two nests per flock and all the birds of the flock help to feed the chicks. One nest at Peterhouse had no less than nine adults feeding three chicks and on a number of occasions the adults were actually queueing up to feed the chicks in the nest.

92 GROUND-SCRAPER THRUSH (R.557)
Plate 22   *TURDUS LITSIPSIRUPA*

Field characters: The boldly spotted breast is probably the most obvious field character, but the rapid flight and rather dumpy appearance are also useful guides. The call is characteristic and the specific name *litsipsirupa* is an onomatopoeic one for the call.

Distribution: This thrush is widely distributed over most of Zimbabwe in suitable areas of well developed woodland. The birds are local in distribution and seem to be restricted by areas of suitable woodland.

Notes: The Ground-scraper Thrush is a rather noisy bird in the early morning and late evening when it sits on the top of a tree and calls for up to half an hour or three-quarters of an hour at a time. It spends a lot of its day searching for food on the ground, merely flying up into the nearest tree at the first sign of danger. The nest is placed in the fork of a tree, usually fairly high up and, in fact, I do not think I have ever found a nest under three metres from the ground.

93 LONG-BILLED CROMBEC (R.621)
Plate 21   *SYLVIETTA RUFESCENS*

Field characters: This warbler is readily distinguishable by the short tail and once the call is known this is also distinctive and a very good field guide. The call consists of a series of rather shrill notes which might be written 'Richi-chichi-chichirrr'.

Distribution: This species is very widespread in Zimbabwe occurring in almost any type of woodland, but is particularly common in the miombo and acacia woodlands.

Notes: If clearly seen, the short tail makes this warbler one which anybody can identify, but warblers seldom allow you to have a very good look as they are always on the move searching for insects. They are usually seen creeping around amongst the foliage of trees rather than lower down. They are typically found in bird parties in winter and can often be heard calling under these circumstances. The nest, as can be seen from the photograph on plate 21, is a neat purse shaped structure suspended near the edge of a tree at no great height above the ground. The bird has to sit with its throat up against the back of the nest in order to get into it. This position looks most uncomfortable, but the bird obviously prefers it.

94 BLACK FLYCATCHER (R.664)
Plate 23   *MELAENORNIS PAMMELAINA*

Field characters: The Black Flycatcher is another wholly black bird which is distinguishable by the slightly forked tail and brown eye (see plate 23). Its habits are also useful guides to identification (see below).

Distribution: This bird occurs over most of Zimbabwe where suitable woodland is found.

Notes: Unlike the Fork-tailed Drongos, Black Flycatchers like to sit on a branch fairly near the ground, preferably under the main part of the tree, from which they can pounce on insects on the ground below. They do catch insects in the air, but most of their food is taken on the ground. They are normally found in pairs although in winter parties of three, four, or five do occur, probably being the adults and chicks of the year. They are generally rather quiet birds although they do have a soft musical song which is uttered at times. The nest is normally placed in a hole in a tree or tree trunk and where suitable holes occur they may be used year after year. The nest shown in the plate was used for at least three consecutive years by a pair of Black Flycatchers.

95 WHITE-FLANKED BATIS (R.673) *BATIS MOLITOR*
Plate 21

Field characters: The call notes are distinctive and are often heard. The male has a three or four syllable whistle which may be rendered 'Chee cher cher' or 'Chee chee cher cher', while the female answers with a rattling or buzzing call (the 'chee' is somewhat lower than the 'cher'). The striking black and white plumage and the russet breast and throat of the female make the batis relatively easy to identify.

Distribution: This species occurs throughout Zimbabwe wherever there is suitable woodland habitat.

Notes: The White-flanked Batis spends much of its time systematically searching the leaves for insects, but will not hesitate to snap up the odd flying insect if the opportunity offers. The birds keep in touch by the calls mentioned above. Once again they are often found in bird parties in the winter and again the call notes will draw attention to the bird at this time. The nest is a very neat cup, normally covered with pieces of lichen which act as an excellent camouflage.

96 BLACK-CROWNED TCHAGRA (R.715)

Plate 23   *TCHAGRA SENEGALA*

Field characters: The red wings, black crown, and hooked bill are all useful field characters. The call is a series of liquid whistles which rise and fall throughout the call.

Distribution: The Black-crowned Tchagra is normally found throughout Zimbabwe in the more scrubby areas or where there is good grass cover beneath the trees.

Notes: The tchagras are generally rather skulking birds, although the Black-crowned is perhaps the boldest of the tchagra species. They spend most of their time searching the bushes near the ground for insects and will even hunt on the ground at times. They are rather slow, heavy fliers and usually glide when this is practical. The nest is a shallow basin of rootlets placed fairly low down in a bush or small tree and is not particularly well concealed. The eggs are white with spots and scrolls of light brown, mauve and grey.

97 WHITE HELMET SHRIKE (R.727)

Plate 23   *PRIONOPS PLUMATA*

Field characters: These birds are always found in small to large parties and their black and white plumage and the rather light, floating flight are distinctive. The yellow eye is obvious only if the birds are seen clearly. They are tame, confiding birds and usually allow fairly close approach which makes study of them easy.

Distribution: Found throughout Zimbabwe in woodland areas, White Helmet Shrikes do not hesitate to move into gardens even in the urban areas. They do not remain in any one place for long as they move around searching for insects.

Notes: The birds are usually seen as they float down from the trees onto the ground where they hop around searching for food. The birds leap-frog one another by making short flights before hopping around again. They keep in contact with a soft chattering call which is not noticed unless you are listening for it. The nest (see photograph on plate 23) is one of the neatest of all those built by southern African birds. The whole nest is covered and smoothed over with spider web and the cup is an almost perfect circle as the bird turns round and round in it while making it. It would appear to be one which is easily spotted and yet it seems to blend in very well with the branch on which it is placed.

98 VIOLET-BACKED OR PLUM-COLOURED STARLING (R.736) *CINNYRICINCLUS LEUCOGASTER*
Plate 23

Field characters: The purple back and head contrasting with the white belly make the male easy to identify. The female is the same shape as the male and is brownish on top and heavily streaked below. The pattern of flight and the bird's rather pointed wings are also a useful guide.

Distribution: The Plum-coloured Starling is a summer visitor to the plateau but is found in the lower lying areas throughout the year.

Notes: These starlings are very partial to mulberries and large numbers may gather at mulberry trees when these are in fruit. The birds nest during the early summer, the eggs being laid in a natural hole in a tree or old woodpecker holes. After nesting, the birds gather into flocks which move around the woodland areas feeding. They may appear very briefly in an area and then seem

to disappear. In flight they have a relatively fast wing beat and
the wings appear to be much more pointed than those of other
starlings in our area. They have a melodious whistling call which
can be heard as they fly overhead.

99 GOLDEN-BREASTED BUNTING (R.874)
Plate 14   *EMBERIZA FLAVIVENTRIS*

Field characters: The striped head and yellow breast are the
main field characters. Note that there is a white stripe both
above and below the eye which distinguishes this species from
the Cabanis' Bunting. The call, described below, is also distinctive.

Distribution: This species is widespread and common in
woodland throughout Zimbabwe being more plentiful in the
lower areas.

Notes: The Golden-breasted Bunting, although inhabiting
woodland, generally feeds on the ground and can be seen walking
along with a rather rolling gait. In the drier areas these buntings
may gather in large numbers to drink at suitable pools or wells.
They do not arive *en masse*, but individuals come and go almost
continually during the morning. They have a rather reedy call,
'Zreede', which has remarkable carrying power considering it
appears to be so soft when you are near the bird. The beautiful
eggs are unusual in that they have a ring of black scrolls and
squiggles at the thick end.

Acacia woodland

The acacia woodlands are essentially in the western part of Zimbabwe, but isolated patches of acacia can be found in the east, on the Mashonaland plateau in the middle of areas of miombo woodland. Where these patches occur you will immediately find different species such as the Long-tailed Shrike appearing in areas where they would not perhaps normally be expected. In the west quite a number of the species listed in the previous chapter will also find their way into acacia because the miombo is less widespread. The acacia woodlands, like the miombo, vary from tall mature woodlands to very short scrub. Over-grazing often plays an important part in determining the degree of present development of this type of woodland and this in turn can affect the bird species present.

The areas of acacia usually show a considerable thickening of the woodland towards the rivers and in fact I think one can normally expect to find considerably more bird life along the rivers than in the drier areas between the rivers, if acacia is the dominant plant type. It would appear, however, that the Crimson-breasted Shrike, for example, requires no water and therefore can be expected to occur anywhere over the acacia areas. Certainly when visiting a new area where acacia occurs I would tend to concentrate on the river valleys unless I had plenty of time to spare to study the area as a whole. Once again bird calls are useful although I find that in the acacia many of the bird calls are perhaps not as readily identifiable as those of the miombo woodlands.

I think that the most abiding memories you will have of acacia areas are the thorns. When you wish to still-hunt, i.e. sit quietly and watch the birds in an area, there always seem to be plenty of thorns to jab you. No sooner do you settle yourself than another thorn makes itself felt and it is therefore often quite difficult to sit still and not disturb the birds. I imagine from the birds' point of view the thorns must be a very useful defence and a deterrent to many of the predators of their nests. Nevertheless, the acacia areas can be extremely interesting and you can expect to find plenty of bird life provided there is a reasonable cover of acacia species.

100 PIED BARBET (R.432)   *LYBIUS LEUCOMELAS*
Plate 25

Field characters: The Pied Barbet has the typically heavy barbet bill although the bill is not as heavy as some of the other species. The dark eyestripe and yellow spots on the back are probably the best field characters if clearly seen. The loud call draws attention to the bird and is also a very good field character. The call is a bi-syllabic 'Pehp-pehp'.

Distribution: Pied Barbets occur over much of central and western Zimbabwe wherever thornveld is found. They do move into the adjacent woodlands, particularly mopane.

Notes: This rather noisy bird is not particularly afraid of man and does not hesitate to come down to see what he is doing. It is always on the move and when flying has a rapid direct flight path from one tree to the next. It is not often seen clinging to the bark of a tree, except at the entrance to the nest hole as in the photograph on plate 25. The nest is excavated in a dead acacia stump with the hole facing downwards in order to keep out the rain.

101 CRIMSON-BREASTED SHRIKE (R.711)
Plate 26   *LANIARIUS ATROCOCCINEUS*

Field characters: From the back this shrike is somewhat similar to the Boubou and Fiscal Shrikes as it has a black back with a white V, but from the front the startlingly red underparts immediately distinguish it. Also, it occurs in a habitat which is not normally favoured by the other two species.

Distribution: This species is confined to the acacia areas of the south-west of Zimbabwe.

Notes: This beautiful bird is interesting in that at night the red breast glows like a stop sign in the lights of a car. It is somewhat localised in occurrence as it sticks very closely to acacia areas, mainly areas with fairly thick growth. It spends a lot of time hopping about on the ground in search of insects, but flies up into a tree at the first sign of danger. It would appear that these birds never need to drink water as they probably obtain sufficient moisture from the insects they eat. The nest is a shallow basin of rather coarse strips of grass, bark, and so on, placed in the fork of an acacia tree, and is not particularly well concealed.

102 LONG-TAILED SHRIKE (R.724)
Plate 25   *CORVINELLA MELANOLEUCUS*

Field characters: This is the only shrike with a very long tail. The black and white plumage and the rather raucous call are also distinctive.

Distribution: Long-tailed Shrikes are found over most of Zimbabwe, but are limited by the occurrence of acacia. In Mashonaland groups of birds are found associated with isolated pockets of acacia woodland in the middle of the miombo.

Notes: They are usually found in pairs or small parties which keep in contact with a whistling call. They are noisy birds which call to one another a great deal and at times the whole group will call in unison. They fly with their tails trailing directly behind them and do not dip down towards the ground as often as other shrikes are inclined to do. They are usually seen perched on a prominent stick from which they pounce on insects below. The basin shaped nest is usually placed near the end of a horizontal branch in a thorn tree.

103 WHITE-CROWNED SHRIKE (R.730)
Plate 26   *EUROCEPHALUS ANGUITINENS*

Field characters: The peculiar whirring flight is the best field character. The bird flies along with the wings apparently held nearly horizontally, merely whirring them up and down at a very great rate. The bird gives the appearance of being rather heavy both in body and head. The call is also a useful guide.

Distribution: Like the Long-tailed Shrike it is very localised in the east, but more widespread in the west.

Notes: The White-crowned Wood Shrike is often seen perched on the outer branches of trees particularly in park-like thornveld. The bird shown in the photograph on plate 26 is the only one I have ever seen which would feed directly from the nest. While brooding, the bird would watch the ground below and, when it saw an insect, drop to the ground, catch the insect, and then return to the nest to feed the chicks. Birds feeding chicks usually tend to collect insects some distance from the nest and then return to the nest with a certain degree of caution. Once again they are rather noisy birds which often draw attention to themselves by their call.

104 RED-SHOULDERED GLOSSY STARLING (R.737)
Plate 25   *LAMPROTORNIS NITENS*

Field characters: The uniform greenish blue and generally darker appearance distinguish this species from the other two similar ones. The call is also different, being a bi-syllabic 'Turr-weeu'.

Distribution: These starlings are common in the west becoming progressively rarer eastwards as far as Harare.

Notes: This species has a very noisy flight because the wings creak with each beat. It is normally found in pairs or in family parties, but larger flocks are sometimes found. These starlings may gather in fair numbers at waterholes to drink. They like to sit on prominent perches on the tops of thorn trees and are thus conspicuous where they occur. When feeding they run around on the ground, but return to the trees as soon as there is any sign of danger. The birds will nest in almost any suitable hole in a tree, fencing pole, or even under eaves of houses. Like other Glossy Starlings they seem to favour the sloughed skins of snakes as well as grass for lining their nests.

105 VIOLET-EARED WAXBILL (R.840)
Plate 14   *URAEGINTHUS GRANATINA*

Field characters: The long tail and the chocolate and purple colours on the head and neck readily distinguish this species. It is altogether a very handsome bird.

Distribution: The Violet-eared Waxbill is found mainly in the west particularly where associations of acacia or burkea occur, but is known as far eastwards as Headlands and the Save river where it is much less common. It is often found in gardens and is attracted to bird tables.

Notes: The Violet-eared Waxbill is, I think, far less easily tamed than the Blue Waxbill, and yet I have found it in some cases to be remarkably tame. It is usually found in pairs or occasionally in small groups and it may join up with the Blue Waxbills. When the bird is disturbed and flies away from you the dark violet rump and heavy tail are most noticeable. The nest is typical of the waxbills, being a ball of fine grass with an entrance which protrudes upwards on one side. It is usually placed at no great height above the ground. The eggs are pure white and the birds are parasitised by the Shaft-tailed Whydah whose chicks are reared together with the waxbill's chicks.

Mopane

The mopane areas are interesting in that you will generally find that once mopane takes over an area, all other species disappear. Mopane seems to exhibit two basic types, either in the form of scrub mopane roughly two metres high, or well developed woodland with tall mopane trees and comparatively barren ground between them.

The scrub mopane is on the whole a rather uninteresting habitat from the bird point of view and there are comparatively few species commonly occurring within it. However, mopane woodlands are very interesting in that they have numerous holes in the older trees which can be used as nest sites by a large variety of bird species. Not surprisingly, therefore, one finds that the birds of the mopane areas are often hole nesting types. The Red-billed and Yellow-billed Hornbills are typical of the mopane in Zimbabwe and there are a large number of other species as well.

Mopane areas are fairly uninteresting to look at in that they lack a variety of tree species, but you should not neglect them in any area which you visit as they do contain quite a large variety of birds, a few of which are described below.

106 DOUBLE-BANDED SANDGROUSE (R.310)
Plate 27 *PTEROCLES BICINCTUS*

Field characters: The typical sandgrouse shape and particularly the shape in flight distinguish this species. The male is easily identified in Zimbabwe by the black and white bands across the chest and forehead. The female has a very finely barred breast and belly with a plain back.

Distribution: This is essentially a bird of the lower lying parts of Zimbabwe and drier west. It is absent from the plateau east of KweKwe.

Notes: This species, unlike others which drink during the day, drinks just after sunset or just before dawn. The birds begin to arrive in small groups just before it is dark. They land some distance from the water and immediately give their gobbling call. They then walk towards the water in a series of short bursts with frequent stops to call again and again. As more and more birds arrive so the volume of calling increases until the waterhole sounds like a popular bar at cocktail time. The birds spend a short time drinking once they reach the water, and then burst up and away with a tremendous clattering of wings. Gradually, as more and more birds leave, the calling dies down until the waterhole falls silent about half an hour after the first birds arrived. During the day they can be found in areas of open mopane where, if disturbed, they rise from almost beneath your feet. They usually fly only a short distance before alighting. In flight the sandgrouse has a very pronounced 'chest' and the wings are rather pointed.

107 RED-BILLED HORNBILL (R.425)
Plate 27   *TOCKUS ERYTHRORHYNCHUS*

Field characters: This species has the smallest bill of any of our hornbills. The comparatively thin red bill combined with the black and white plumage makes identification easy. The call is also characteristic.

Distribution: This bird is common over much of the lower parts of Zimbabwe, but mainly in areas of mopane.

Notes: The Red-billed Hornbill seems to spend a lot of its time walking on the ground with a rather peculiar rolling action. It is often seen perched on the outer branches of a tree from which it surveys the surrounding countryside. It is normally found in small flocks and often occurs in association with the Yellow-billed Hornbill. In many parts of the country it has become very tame, particularly in game reserve camps. Like most of the hornbills the female is sealed in the nest and fed by the male until the chicks are roughly half grown.

108 YELLOW-BILLED HORNBILL (R.426)
Plate 31   *TOCKUS FLAVIROSTRIS*

Field characters: Although at first glance similar to the Red-billed Hornbill, it is a larger bird and the bill is heavier looking (see plate 31). The bill is yellow not red, but this may not always be obvious in the field. The call, often uttered by the whole flock in unison, is a series of 'Tocks' repeated rapidly for about twenty to thirty seconds.

Distribution: Although very widespread in the mopane, this species is often found in other habitats. It is seldom found above 1 300 to 1 500 metres above sea level.

Notes: Like the Red-billed species the birds spend much of their time searching for food on the ground, but they also clamber around in the trees searching for berries and insects. They become quite tame when in association with man provided they are not disturbed. They usually greet the dawn with a cacophony of calling and it seems that different groups try to outdo one another.

Forests

The true forests are limited to the eastern parts of Zimbabwe mainly within the mountains of Nyanga and the Chimanimanis. The trees are evergreens and may grow to a very considerable height forming a continuous canopy which is strengthened by the presence of a variety of creepers and epiphytes. The forests are interesting in that you will find in them a number of species which are widespread and common in the Cape, but which are severely restricted in Zimbabwe. The big problem here is to get a good look at the birds as most of them tend to stay within the forest itself where the light is not necessarily very good. Many of the species are fairly noisy and most have distinctive calls, but as in reed beds it is often extremely frustrating trying to find out what bird is making a particular call within the forest canopy.

The species which occur commonly within the forest may occur as far west as Marondera. However, these species are on the whole only really common within the areas of moist evergreen forest.

109 OLIVE THRUSH (R.553)   *TURDUS OLIVACEUS*
Plate 29

Field characters: The Olive Thrush has a rather plump body and is generally dark in colour. The back is a dark brown while the breast and belly are a dark olive green and the throat is more or less streaked with dark brown. The bill is a yellowish colour and this immediately distinguishes it from the Kurrichane Thrush.

Distribution: This is essentially a bird of the forests of the Eastern Districts, but it may be seen quite commonly in areas bordering forests. It has been recorded as far west as Marondera.

Notes: Because this species lives in the rain forests it is often difficult to get a really good view of the bird and this may complicate identification. However, they do venture out from the forest particularly in the early morning and late evening and will also come to bird tables and bird baths if suitable food is put out. They spend most of their time on the ground and like all the thrushes they are very good runners. They usually run a few metres and then stop to look around in case of danger. They will scratch around in dead leaves looking for food as they feed mostly on insects, although they will also eat fruit when it is available.

110 CAPE ROBIN (R.581)   *COSSYPHA CAFFRA*
Plate 29

Field characters: This robin is probably most easily identified in the field by its call which may be rendered 'Jan-fred-erik'. The orange throat and grey belly (see plate 29) are also characteristic as other similar robins in our area have the orange going right down on to the belly. The white eye-stripe is usually obvious, but this is not a very good field character, as a number of other robins also have this stripe. When the bird flies away, the reddish brown rump and outer tail feathers are usually fairly obvious and this is a good guide to many of the robin species.

Distribution: A bird of the forests and bush of the east the Cape Robin extends westwards at least as far as Marondera where I have found it breeding at about 1 500 metres in thick bush along a river.

Notes: Cape Robins are early risers and their clear calls can be heard from first light in the Inyanga mountains. They usually call from within, but near the top of, a tree or bush and will sing continuously for an hour or more in the morning. They also call late into the evening often continuing even when it is pitch dark. The nest is a mass of sticks and finer material with a neat cup in the centre lined with fine rootlets or grasses. It is usually placed fairly near the ground and is often against a bank where it can be concealed by overhanging vegetation. The birds sit very still and allow a close approach when there are eggs or young chicks.

111 CAPE BATIS (R.672)   *BATIS CAPENSIS*
Plate 28

Field characters: The very broad black chest band of the male and russet flanks are usually very obvious, while the female has the whole of the throat, breast, and most of the belly russet coloured. They have a call which is similar to that of the White-flanked Batis which may be written as 'Reep-reep-reep'.

Distribution: The Cape Batis is restricted to the forest areas of the Eastern Districts and the thicker woodlands of the Matopos area.

Notes: The Cape Batis is a common resident species of the forests and does not generally overlap with the White-flanked Batis except in the Matopos or possibly the extreme western part of the eastern highlands. These birds are extremely active, forever on the move, hopping around through the branches of the trees in which they live. The nest is a very beautiful cup shaped one which is not usually particularly well hidden, but as breeding occurs within forests the gloom probably helps to keep the nest from sight. While sitting, the birds are extremely tame and I have on occasion been able to stroke the back of a female sitting on eggs. They are fairly noisy birds and once their various calls are known one soon realises that they are quite common in the forests.

112 EAST AFRICAN SWEE (R.826)
Plate 30   *ESTRILDA MELANOTIS*

Field characters: The swees are some of our smallest birds and are usually seen scratching around on open ground near thick bush or forests in the Eastern Districts. They are easily identified because of their orange rump and if clearly seen the yellow belly and grey head are also useful field characters.

Distribution: They are found in the Eastern Highlands in association with forest or thick bush. A different subspecies in which the males have black faces is also found in the Matopos and near Great Zimbabwe.

Notes: Swees usually occur in small flocks which move around in search of grass or other fine seeds, feeding essentially on the ground. The birds in the flock keep in contact with a very quiet 'Swee' call. The nest is a pear shaped one made of fine grass stems which point upwards at one side to form the entrance.

Open mountain

The Eastern Districts have large areas of mountainous terrain which is characterised by heath-covered slopes and many rocky outcrops. This type of habitat may be considered to extend westwards in the form of granite dwalas, but species such as the Blue Swallow will not be found here as they are restricted to the true mountains of the east. Many of the birds of this habitat are those which spend a lot of time gliding or flying slowly above the mountains making use of the numerous air currents caused by the rising land. The smaller birds tend to be restricted to a much greater extent and are controlled by the presence or absence of the various habitats. These areas are generally rather moist, and rain and certainly mist can occur throughout the year.

113 AUGUR BUZZARD (R.153)
Plate 24   *BUTEO RUFOFUSCUS AUGUR*

Field characters: This beautiful dark brown and white bird with the rufous tail should be easily identified by anybody who sees it in the Eastern Districts. It has a loud ringing call which has been likened by some authors to that of the jackal. In flight the white line under the wings is usually very obvious and is distinctive.

Distribution: The Augur Buzzard is really common only in the mountainous areas of the Eastern Districts, but it may occur in rocky country westwards right through to Matabeleland.

Notes: Augur Buzzards are often seen circling overhead riding the air currents associated with the mountains. They will frequently be heard calling; the loud ringing cries can be heard at a considerable distance and draw attention to the bird. They nest either on ledges on cliffs or, where such suitable nest sites are not available, on or near the tops of large trees.

Field characters: In flight the lack of white on the belly and the heavy bill and head are usually the best field characters. The wings are generally broader and more rounded than those of birds of prey. The raven is a much heavier bird than the Pied Crow and the call, a deep throated 'Kraak', is also distinctive.

Distribution: The White-necked Raven is found over most of Zimbabwe wherever suitable rocky outcrops occur. It is a very wide-ranging bird and may therefore appear almost anywhere, but will generally return to kopjes or mountains to roost.

Notes: These birds are scavengers and use their strong heavy bills to tear pieces of meat off dead animals such as hares killed on the roads at night. They have been known to eat fruit as well. They nest on ledges on cliffs usually in the most inaccessible places. Unfortunately they are known to be predatory on chickens kept in confined runs and have even been known to kill lambs or sick sheep. They are very wary birds and in spite of considerable persecution have been able to survive in fairly large numbers throughout most of southern Africa.

115 MALACHITE SUNBIRD (R.751)

Plate 24   *NECTARINIA FAMOSA*

Field characters: The male is easily distinguishable because of its metallic green colour and long tail feathers. It might be confused with the Bronze Sunbird, but the difference in colour is such that confusion is rather unlikely. The female on the other hand is more difficult to distinguish and is easily confused with the female of the Bronze Sunbird because of the similar size. The bill is generally longer, however, and less curved than that of the female Bronze Sunbird. It also lacks the white eyebrow.

Distribution: It is confined to the mountains of the east above about 1 000 metres.

Notes: The Malachite Sunbird is an easily recognised species and is soon recorded in areas where it occurs. The males spend much time sitting on conspicuous perches from which they chase other males or even other sunbirds. This bird, like other sunbirds, prefers to feed at plants having tubular flowers, but the Malachite Sunbird also hawks insects flying past its perch. The nest is a fairly typical one, but it is usually placed near water.

Rocky outcrop

The rocky outcrops in Zimbabwe vary from the smooth, rounded granite dwalas or exfoliation domes through the balancing rocks to fairly typical cliffs in well jointed rocks such as quartzites. The rocks form nesting havens for a number of species most of which tend to feed in the surrounding countryside or at least in the limited vegetation associated with the rocks. The birds are essentially either predators or insectivorous and it is interesting to note how many of the smaller birds such as the Rock Nightjar feed on the wing. The rocks form a suitable nesting habitat for a number of species such as the Rock Kestrels. Other species which nest on the rocks are probably better included under other habitats as they are normally associated with particular habitats, such as the miombo woodland in the case of the Lesser Striped Swallow. In most cases the need for overhanging rocks or crevices in the rocks suitable for nest sites is important and thus the true bald dwalas tend to be of less interest than the more broken pieces of rock. The Matopos, which at first glance appears to be an area of purely rounded exfoliation domes, is in fact an excellent area because of the presence of numerous ledges, cracks, and crevices suitable both as nesting sites and also, in the case of the Black Eagles, as a retreat for their main prey, the dassie. The Black Eagles in the Matopos are in fact exceptional and we have here one of the greatest, if not the greatest, breeding concentrations of large raptors in the world. On the other hand the Boulder Chat is found associated only with rocky outcrops within the miombo woodlands and probably relies as much on the woodlands as the rocks in determination of habitat. Where the rocky outcrops are of limited size you can expect to find birds from woodlands in the immediate vicinity and from surrounding grasslands.

116 ROCK KESTREL (R.123)   *FALCO TINNUNCULUS*
Plate 32

Field characters: The Rock Kestrel is probably best identified by the bluish head, but also by the fact that it is generally more reddish in colour than other falcons or kestrels which might be seen in a similar habitat.

Distribution: Although the Rock Kestrel may appear almost anywhere it is essentially a bird of rocky areas and seldom goes far from its chosen territory.

Notes: Rock Kestrels are very local birds and spend most of their time in the vicinity of the rocky area in their individual territories. They are usually found in pairs and may be seen sitting on pinnacles of rock or other vantage points from which they are able to survey the surrounding areas. They are often seen gliding or hanging almost motionless in the updraught at the edge of a cliff or rock face. They normally nest on ledges or in holes in cliffs. They feed essentially on insects, small rodents and reptiles and possibly take the occasional bird.

117 BLACK EAGLE (R.133)   *AQUILA VERREAUXII*
Plate 18

Field characters: This is a very large black eagle with a very noticeable white back. In flight the outer third of the wings is light in colour, appearing almost white with black bars.

Distribution: The Black Eagle is very widespread in Zimbabwe, but localised because it is always associated with rocky outcrops.

Notes: The Black Eagle feeds essentially on dassies (Rock Hyrax) and is therefore found only where these are common. In the Matopos we have one of the largest and most dense breeding populations of Black Eagles in Africa. The birds are often seen sitting on prominent perches near the tops of kopjes or rocky areas, or else may be seen riding the air currents associated with the varying terrain found in these areas. The nest is a large mass of sticks placed on a ledge on a cliff face. If the bird lays two eggs, one being the normal clutch, then only one chick will survive as the larger of the two will kill the smaller one. When hunting, the Black Eagle apparently comes round the corner of a cliff or over

the top of a cliff and hits its prey before the latter has time to dive
for cover.

118 ROCK PIGEON (R.311)   *COLUMBA GUINEA*
Plate 32

Field characters: The Rock Pigeon has a typical dove or pigeon
shape and is the largest of the pigeons or doves commonly
found in Zimbabwe. The generally mauvish or reddish colour
combined with the large patch of bare red skin around the eye
and the spots on the wings distinguish this species quite readily.

Distribution: The Rock Pigeon, in the wild, is confined to
areas of rocky outcrops with steep cliffs and crevices. It has
adapted to man's cities and is therefore often found in areas
where there are plenty of large buildings with suitable nesting
sites under the eaves or on ledges.

Notes: Outside the main towns the Rock Pigeon is somewhat
localised in occurrence, but it may be seen in almost any piece of
rocky country, particularly rocky kopjes with extensive areas of
balancing rocks, or where there are fairly large cliffs with ledges
and cracks. It has become quite common in certain urban areas
and can be a real pest in that it dirties buildings both with its
droppings and its very untidy nests. When seen at close quarters
the Rock Pigeon is a very handsome bird and it will come to
feed at bird tables.

119 SPOTTED EAGLE OWL (R.368) *BUBO AFRICANUS*
Plate 31

Field characters: The smallest of the eagle owls in Zimbabwe, it
is generally best identified by its call which is a bi-syllabic 'Hoo-
hoo'. The female may answer with a tri-syllabic 'Hoo-oo
hoo'. The underparts are barred and the bird has two feather
tufts or 'ears' on the head.

Distribution: The Spotted Eagle Owl is found throughout
Zimbabwe wherever rocks are encountered, but may also inhabit
woodland areas.

Notes: Spotted Eagle Owls are often seen sitting on top of
roadside telephone posts and in fact are often seen on the road at

night where large numbers are killed by motor cars. They are common in most areas and can be heard calling at almost any time of the year. They probably feed mainly on insects although small rodents and reptiles are taken when the opportunity offers. They nest on ledges on almost any rocky outcrop, but will also nest in mines, wells, houses, hollow trees, and on top of other birds' nests such as the Hamerkop's if no suitable ledge is available. I have even found them nesting between rocks on the bare ground. They are usually found sitting in a sheltered nook or up against the trunk of a tree during the day.

120 FRECKLED or ROCK NIGHTJAR (R.374)
Plate 32   *CAPRIMULGUS TRISTIGMA*

Field characters: The call which may have two, three, or four syllables is a rather breathless 'Whow-whow'. The bird, is very much greyer than other species and is obviously barred and therefore easily distinguished. The habitat is also of great importance.

Distribution: The Freckled or Rock Nightjar occurs over the whole of Zimbabwe wherever suitable rocky outcrops are found.

Notes: This species usually occurs where one finds outcrops of granite, particularly in areas where there are large dwalas or in the balancing rocks in the middle of miombo woodland. Unless disturbed it is always found sitting in the open on bare rocks and the photograph on plate 32 shows clearly how well the bird is camouflaged against this background. The eggs are laid in a hollow near the top of a rock. They are light grey in colour and therefore resemble pieces of lichen. Like all nightjars the Freckled Nightjar relies on its excellent camouflage to escape detection and will let you walk right up to it without flying away.

121 BOULDER CHAT (R.538) *PINARORNIS PLUMOSUS*
Plate 26

Field characters: The uniform sooty brown colour with white tips to the outer three tail feathers is distinctive. The call which sounds rather like an unoiled wheelbarrow being pushed along is also characteristic and draws attention to the bird when it might otherwise be missed.

Distribution: The Boulder Chat is found over much of Zimbabwe wherever suitable rocky, boulder-strewn areas occur, usually with woodland associated with the rocks.

Notes: Your attention is usually drawn to the bird by the loud squeaky call mentioned above. It is very much at home on rocks and seems able to run up even very steep rocks with minimal use of its wings. These chats are not normally found on areas of bare rock and they do not hesitate to move into the trees above their chosen habitat. Like many of the other chats and robins this species raises and lowers its tail following each movement.

Index

Cormorant, Reed	30	42	8
Coucal, Senegal = Fleck's	47	56	9
Crake, Black	44	53	9
Crane, Crowned	52	61	4
Crombec, Long-billed	93	98	21
Crow, Pied	5	17	—
Dabchick, Cape	29	41	7
Darter	31	43	8
Dove, Cape Turtle	80	89	19
Dove, Laughing	2	15	27
Dove, Namaqua	72	80	19
Dove, Red-eyed	1	14	11
Drongo, Fork-tailed	87	94	20
Duck, Knob-billed	33	44	8
Duck, White-faced	42	52	17
Eagle, Black	117	119	18
Eagle, Fish	35	45	18
Eagle, Martial	77	86	18
Egret, Cattle	59	69	17
Firefinch, Jameson's	13	25	2
Flycatcher, Black	94	98	23
Flycatcher, Paradise	20	32	5
Francolin, Swainson's	43	53	31
Goose, Egyptian	41	51	8
Grebe, Little = Dabchick	29	41	7
Guineafowl, Crowned	79	88	17
Hamerkop	40	50	4
Harrier, African Marsh	51	61	31
Heron, Grey	32	44	12
Hoopoe, African	15	28	5
Hornbill, Grey	83	91	—
Hornbill, Red-billed	107	109	27
Hornbill, Yellow-billed	108	109	31
Jacana, African	38	47	6
Kestrel, Rock	116	119	32
Kingfisher, Malachite	49	57	7
Kingfisher, Pied	48	56	6
Kite, Black	61	70	4
Kite, Black-shouldered	70	78	—
Kite, Yellow-billed	61	70	4
Lark, Rufous-naped	63	72	15
Longclaw, Yellow-throated	55	64	7
Lourie, Grey	73	81	—
Mannikin, Bronze	12	24	1
Marsh Harrier	51	61	31
Moorhen, Common	36	46	6
Mousebird, Red-faced	4	16	11
Nightjar, Fiery-necked	82	90	19
Nightjar, Rock = Freckled	120	121	32
Oriole, African Golden	88	95	22
Oriole, Black-headed	89	96	20
Owl, Spotted Eagle	119	120	31
Parrot, Meyer's	81	89	19
Pigeon, Rock	118	120	32
Pipit, Buffy	65	73	13
Plover, Blacksmith	45	54	9
Plover, Crowned	62	71	10
Plover, Wattled	53	62	10
Quelea, Red-billed	66	74	16
Raven, White-necked	114	116	—
Robin, Cape	110	112	29
Robin, Heuglin's	7	19	13